DJI Mini 5 Pro Pilot's Hardware Handbook

Master Every Component, Controller Operation & Pre-Flight Setup—The Complete Hardware Guide for Beginners

Sammy Addy

Master Every Component, Controller Operation & Pre-Flight Setup—The Complete Hardware Guide for Beginners 1
Disclaimer 7
Chapter 1 8
Understanding Your DJI Mini 5 Pro - What You Have in Your Box 8
What Is Inside Your Box 8
Understanding the Drone's Physical Layout 11
Understanding the Remote Controller Layout 15
Understanding the Batteries 19
Propeller Safety and Storage 21
The Gimbal Protector 22
Charging Equipment Overview 22
Chapter 2 23
Your First Unboxing & Pre-Flight Assembly 23
Step-by-Step Unboxing 23
Removing Protective Film 24
Attaching Propellers 25
Installing Batteries 26
Control Stick Installation 27
Unfolding the Drone 28
Powering On Sequence 29
Visual Inspection before First Flight 31
Chapter 3 33
The DJI Fly App - Getting Started 33
Downloading & Installing 33

Chapter 11 137

All the Cables, Connectors & What They Do 137

- USB-C Main Cable 137
- Micro-USB vs USB-C: 138
- Propeller Removal Tool 140
- ND Filters 142
- Gimbal Protector 145
- microSD Card 147
- Spare Parts Kit Organization 149

Chapter 12 156

Firmware Updates & Maintenance 156

- What is Firmware? 156
- How to Update 158
- Update Process 160
- Battery Firmware 162
- Controller Firmware 163
- Cleaning Routine 165
- Storage Maintenance 167
- When to Contact Support 169

Disclaimer

This book is intended for **educational and informational purposes only**. While every effort has been made to ensure the accuracy and reliability of the information provided, the author makes no guarantees regarding the completeness, correctness, or suitability of any content.

Operating a drone, including the DJI Mini 5 Pro, involves **inherent risks**. Readers are solely responsible for their actions, decisions, and safety while using the drone. The author and publisher shall not be held liable for any damage, injury, legal issues, or loss that may occur as a result of using the information in this book.

Drone laws, regulations, and restrictions vary by country and region. It is the reader's responsibility to **understand and comply with all local aviation laws, safety guidelines, and operational requirements** before flying.

Always follow the official instructions and safety guidelines provided by DJI and consult the official user manual for the DJI Mini 5 Pro.

By using this book, you acknowledge that you are doing so **at your own risk** and accept full responsibility for your drone operations.

Chapter 1

Understanding Your DJI Mini 5 Pro - What You Have in Your Box

What Is Inside Your Box

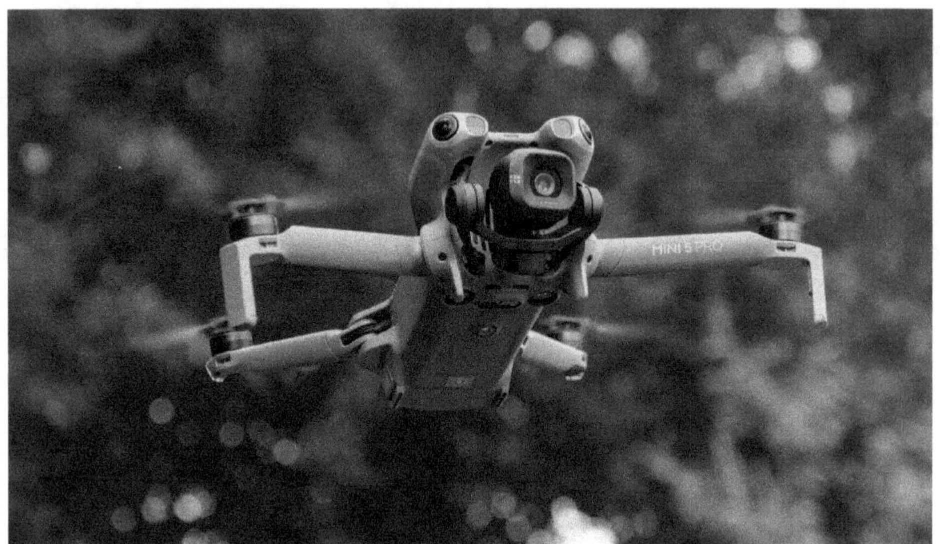

When you first open your DJI Mini 5 Pro box, you'll find several items. Let me explain what each one is and why you need it before you can fly.

The exact contents depend on which package you bought. The most common package is called the "Fly More Kit," which includes the most items. Even if you bought a different package, the main components are the same.

- The DJI Mini 5 Pro Drone Itself

The first and most important item is the drone. At first glance, it looks like a small, folded-up piece of technology. This is the aircraft that will fly in the air. The drone weighs 248 grams, which makes it lightweight enough to carry in your hands, but it's still powerful enough to capture excellent photos and videos.

When you first look at your drone while it's folded, you'll notice it looks compact and rectangular. The front and back have folds, and the sides have arms that stick out. This is the normal way the drone is stored and transported. Everything you see on the outside serves a purpose, and we'll go through each part as we continue.

- The Remote Controller (RC 2)

The second major item is the remote controller, also called the RC 2. This is what you hold in your hands to control the drone while it flies. It looks similar to a game controller, but it has a built-in screen on top and buttons on the back.

The controller has two handles with control sticks that you push to fly the drone. It has buttons on the top and bottom for taking photos and videos. It has dials that you rotate to adjust your camera view. These are the main ways you'll interact with and control your drone.

The controller is powered by a rechargeable battery inside it, and it can last up to three hours of continuous use before needing a charge. This means you can fly multiple battery cycles on the drone without charging the controller.

- The Intelligent Flight Batteries

Your kit comes with either one, two, or three rechargeable batteries (called "Intelligent Flight Batteries"). Each battery powers the drone for roughly 19 to 23 minutes of continuous flying. The exact time depends on weather, your flying style, and how much you're asking the drone to do.

These batteries are smart. They have a built-in computer chip that monitors their health, temperature, and charge level. You'll see LED lights on each battery that tell you how much charge is remaining. The batteries are also designed to warm themselves up if the weather is cold, so you can safely fly in cooler temperatures.

If you have the Fly More Kit, you'll have three batteries total. This means you can fly for about 60 minutes of total flight time if you charge them all fully. Each battery should be fully charged before you use it.

- The Charging Hub

If your kit includes a charging hub (also called a charging station), this is where you charge your batteries. It's a rectangular device with three battery slots and a USB-C charging port on the bottom.

The charging hub has lights that show you the charge status of each battery. When you plug the hub into power, it can charge all three batteries at the same time. Without a hub, you can charge batteries directly through the drone's USB-C port, but the hub is much more convenient if you have multiple batteries.

- The Propellers

Your kit includes spare propellers. The DJI Mini 5 Pro uses four propellers—two for the front and two for the back. The propellers that come in your box are extras for when you need to replace a damaged one. Propellers can get damaged if you crash, hit a tree, or have any accident. Keeping spares on hand means you can quickly replace a broken one and get back to flying. The propellers for the Mini 5 Pro are unique to this model and won't work with other DJI drones.

Propellers come in pairs. Two propellers have a clockwise rotation (they spin one direction), and two have a counterclockwise rotation (they spin the other direction). You cannot mix them up—each one only fits on its specific motor.

- The Gimbal Protector

The gimbal protector is a plastic cover that protects the camera and gimbal system on the front of the drone. The gimbal is the mechanism that stabilizes your camera and allows it to tilt up and down. The camera is very delicate, so the gimbal protector is essential when transporting your drone.

The gimbal protector clips onto the drone's body. It has a tab that you pull down to release it before you fly. Always make sure the protector is removed before powering on the drone.

- Cables and Charging Equipment

Your kit includes at least one USB-C cable. This cable connects to the charging hub and the USB-C charging port on your drone's body. You can also use this cable to charge your controller.

If your kit is the Fly More Kit, you'll also have other cables and possibly adapters. These allow you to charge the equipment using different types of power sources, like USB power adapters or car chargers.

- The Quick Start Guide and Documentation

Your kit includes printed documentation, including a quick start guide. While this guide will help you, this beginner's guide goes into much more depth and explains every feature specifically for the DJI Mini 5 Pro.

Understanding the Drone's Physical Layout

Now that you know what's in your box, let's look at the actual drone and understand the different parts on its body. This will help you navigate the physical hardware.

The Four Arms

The DJI Mini 5 Pro has four arms that fold in and out. These arms are located at the corners of the drone's body.

When you look at the drone from the front, the two arms on the left side fold out to the left, and the two arms on the right side fold out to the right. At the end of each arm is a motor with a propeller attached.

The arms are meant to fold in for storage and transport. When you're ready to fly, you unfold all four arms until they click into a locked position.

This is called "unfolding the drone." The locked position is when the arms are fully extended and perpendicular to the drone's body.

The Four Motors

At the end of each arm is a motor. These are the spinning devices that power the propellers. The motors on the Mini 5 Pro are brushless motors, which means they run silently and efficiently compared to older drone motors.

Each motor has a propeller attached to it. The motors work together to lift the drone into the air and help you steer it. If any motor fails or isn't spinning properly, the drone cannot fly safely.

The Landing Feet

Underneath the drone's body, there are four small landing feet. These are simple rubber or plastic pads that protect the drone's body when it lands on the ground. The landing feet keep the main body elevated slightly, protecting the camera and other sensitive parts from getting damaged.

The landing feet are fixed, which means they don't fold in or out. They're always there. The drone sits on these feet when it lands.

The Camera and Gimbal

On the front of the drone, underneath the body, is the camera system. The camera is mounted on a gimbal, which is a mechanical stabilizer. The gimbal can tilt the camera up and down while the drone is flying, so you can adjust what you're looking at without moving the whole drone.

The camera on the Mini 5 Pro is advanced for such a small drone. It can take high-quality photos and videos. The camera has an autofocus system that automatically keeps your subject sharp.

The gimbal is very delicate. This is why the gimbal protector is so important during transport. Never touch the gimbal system without good reason, and always handle it gently.

The Camera Lens

The camera lens is a small glass piece at the very front of the camera. This is what lets light in to create images. The lens is smooth and can get scratched or dirty.

You should keep the lens clean by gently wiping it with a soft, microfiber cloth. Never use rough materials or liquids on the lens, as this can damage it. If there's dust on the lens, you can blow it gently off with your breath or use a soft brush.

The Sensors

The DJI Mini 5 Pro has several sensors that help it understand its environment and fly safely. These sensors are small cameras located in different parts of the drone:

There are obstacle avoidance cameras on the front of the drone. These cameras look ahead and alert the drone if there's an obstacle in the way, like a tree or building.

There are also obstacle avoidance cameras on the back of the drone, so the drone can detect obstacles behind it if you're flying backward.

Underneath the drone is a downward-facing camera. This camera helps the drone understand how high above the ground it is and helps it land safely.

These sensors are always working in the background. You don't need to do anything to activate them. They're designed to help keep your drone safe.

The Battery Compartment

On the bottom of the drone's body, there's a battery slot. This is where you insert the Intelligent Flight Battery. The battery clicks into this slot and stays secure during flight.

To install a battery, you align it with the slot and press it in until you hear a click. To remove it, you press the release buttons on the sides of the battery and pull it out gently.

You cannot fly the drone without a battery installed. Always make sure the battery is fully inserted and locked in place before powering on.

The Gimbal Protector Attachment Points

The gimbal protector clips onto the drone's body at two points near the camera. There's a tab at the bottom of the gimbal protector that you pull down to release it.

Always make sure the gimbal protector is attached before transporting your drone and removed before flying.

The Power Button

The power button is located on the top of the drone's body, near the rear. It's a small button that you press to turn the drone on and off.

To turn on the drone, you press the power button once, then press and hold it for about two seconds until you hear a beep sound. The drone will then power up and start its self-diagnostic checks.

To turn off the drone, you press the power button once, then press and hold it for about two seconds. You'll hear a beep sound indicating that the drone is shutting down.

The USB-C Port

On the bottom of the drone, near the back, is a USB-C charging port. This is where you plug in the charging cable to charge the battery while it's installed in the drone.

You can also use this port to transfer files (photos and videos) from the drone to your computer, though this is less common because most people use the microSD card instead.

The microSD Card Slot

Next to the USB-C port on the bottom of the drone is a microSD card slot. This is a tiny slot where you insert a microSD memory card. The microSD card stores all your photos and videos.

If you don't have a microSD card, the drone has internal storage, but it's limited. A microSD card gives you much more space to store your footage. microSD cards are inexpensive and can be found at most electronics stores.

To insert a microSD card, you gently push it into the slot until it clicks. To remove it, you push it in slightly until it clicks and pops out.

Understanding the Remote Controller Layout

Now let's look at the remote controller in detail. This is what you hold in your hands to control the drone.

The Power Button

On the remote controller, the power button is located on the back, in the center. It's a small recessed button. To power on the controller, you press it once, then press and hold for about two seconds. You'll hear a beep sound.

To power off, you press it once and hold it for about two seconds. The controller will beep to confirm it's shutting down.

The controller should always be powered on when the drone is flying. If the controller loses power or turns off while the drone is in the air, the drone will try to land itself safely.

The Control Sticks

The control sticks are located at the bottom of the controller, one on each side. They're the two joystick-like sticks that you push in different directions to control the drone's movement.

The left control stick controls the drone's altitude (up and down) and rotation (spinning left or right). The right control stick controls the drone's forward and backward movement and side-to-side movement.

The control sticks come out of the controller and slot into the bottom. When you're not using them, you can remove them by pulling straight out and insert them back into their storage slots when you're done flying. This makes the controller more compact for travel.

The control sticks should move smoothly in all directions. If you feel resistance or grinding, something might be wrong with them. Stop using them and contact support.

The Record Button

On the top-right of the remote controller is the record button. This is a button that you press to start and stop video recording. When you press it once, video recording starts. When you press it again, video recording stops.

There's also a light on or near this button that turns on when you're recording, so you can see at a glance that the drone is capturing video.

The Focus/Shutter Button

To the left of the record button is the focus/shutter button. This button is used for taking photos.

To take a photo, you press this button all the way down. To focus on a subject without taking a photo yet, you press the button halfway down. This is useful if you want to make sure something is sharp before you capture the image.

The Left Dial

Just above the left control stick is a dial (a rotating wheel). This is the left dial, and it controls the gimbal tilt. The gimbal tilt is the vertical angle of your camera—whether it's pointing straight ahead, tilted up toward the sky, or tilted down toward the ground.

To tilt the camera up, you rotate the left dial forward (toward the top of the controller). To tilt the camera down, you rotate the left dial backward (toward the bottom of the controller).

The dial moves smoothly in a full circle. You can rotate it as much as you want. The more you rotate it, the faster the camera tilts.

The Right Dial

Just above the right control stick is another dial. This is the right dial, and it controls zoom. The zoom allows you to make distant objects appear closer.

To zoom in (make things look bigger), you rotate the right dial forward (toward the top of the controller). To zoom out (make things look smaller), you rotate the right dial backward (toward the bottom of the controller).

The Mini 5 Pro has three zoom levels: 1x (normal view), 2x (medium zoom), and 4x (digital zoom). As you rotate the dial, you'll see the zoom level change on the screen.

The Customizable C1 and C2 Buttons

On the back of the remote controller, underneath the left side, is a button labeled C1. Underneath the right side is a button labeled C2. These are customizable buttons.

By default, these buttons control gimbal functions, but you can change what they do through the DJI Fly app settings. This makes them very flexible. We'll learn how to customize these buttons in a later chapter.

The C1 button is on the left side of the back of the controller. The C2 button is on the right side of the back of the controller.

The Return to Home (RTH) Button

In the center of the back of the remote controller is the Return to Home button. This button tells the drone to come back to the location where it took off.

The RTH button is a large, recessed button. To use it, you press and hold the button for a moment. The drone will then automatically return to the takeoff location and land itself.

This is an important safety feature. If you lose control of the drone or the drone loses its connection to the controller, it will automatically return home and land.

The Back Button

Near the top-right of the remote controller's screen is a back button. This button allows you to navigate backward through the app menus on the controller's screen.

If you press it once, you go back one screen. If you press it twice quickly, you return to the home screen.

The Status LED and Battery LEDs

On the back of the remote controller, you'll see several small lights. These are LED indicators.

The status LED shows the current connection state of the controller. If it's green, everything is connected properly. If it's red or blinking, there might be a connection issue.

The battery level LEDs show how much battery power the controller has. These are usually shown as a series of small lights that fill in like a battery indicator on a phone. If only one light is on, the battery is low.

The Touchscreen

The top of the remote controller has a built-in touchscreen. This screen shows you what the drone's camera is seeing in real-time. It also shows you all the app menus and settings where you can configure your drone.

The screen is similar to a tablet or smartphone screen. You tap on it with your fingers to navigate menus and adjust settings.

The screen also displays important flight information, like your altitude, distance from the drone, and battery level.

The Antennas

Sticking up from the top corners of the remote controller are two antennas. These send and receive signals between the controller and the drone. They work automatically, so you don't need to do anything with them, but keep them vertical (pointing straight up) for the best signal quality.

If you travel with the controller, you can fold these antennas down to make it more compact.

The USB-C Charging Port

On the bottom of the remote controller is a USB-C charging port. You can plug in a USB-C cable here to charge the controller's battery.

The controller should be charged before each flying session to ensure you have enough battery power to keep the drone flying safely.

Understanding the Batteries

Now let's understand the Intelligent Flight Batteries in detail.

What Makes These Batteries Special

The batteries in the DJI Mini 5 Pro kit are not ordinary batteries. They have built-in technology that makes them smart. This technology monitors the battery's health, temperature, and charge level in real time.

Each battery has a small computer chip inside that communicates with the drone. The chip tells the drone exactly how much power is available and helps manage the power safely.

The Battery Indicator Lights

On the outside of each battery, there are four small LED lights. These lights tell you how much charge the battery has.

If all four lights are on, the battery is fully charged (100%). If three lights are on, the battery is about 75% charged. If two lights are on, it's about 50% charged. If only one light is on, it's about 25% charged and should be charged soon.

To check the charge level of a battery that's not in the drone, press the small button on the side of the battery. The LED lights will briefly show you the charge level. If no lights come on, the battery is dead and needs to be charged.

Battery Flight Time

Each fully charged battery will give you roughly 19 to 23 minutes of continuous flight time. The exact time depends on several factors:

If you fly on a calm day with no wind, you'll get longer flight time. If you fly on a windy day, the motors have to work harder, and you'll get less flight time.

If you fly aggressively (moving fast and making sharp turns), you use more power and get less flight time. If you fly smoothly and slowly, you get more flight time.

Cold weather reduces battery performance. If it's below 50 degrees Fahrenheit, your flight time will be shorter.

Generally, expect to get about 20 minutes of actual flying per fully charged battery. Always plan your flights to end before the battery is completely empty.

Charging Batteries

To charge the batteries, you have two options. First, you can use the charging hub (if your kit includes one). The hub can charge all three batteries at the same time, which is convenient.

Second, you can charge a battery that's installed in the drone by connecting a USB-C cable to the drone's USB-C port. This works, but it's slower than using the hub.

To use the charging hub, you insert each battery into one of the three slots until it clicks in place. Then you plug the USB-C cable from the hub into a USB power adapter connected to wall power. The hub will begin charging. The hub has lights that show the charge status of each battery. When a battery is fully charged, its light will stop blinking and stay solid.

Important Battery Safety

Never expose the batteries to extreme heat or cold. Don't leave them in a hot car or in freezing temperatures for extended periods. This damages the battery and can cause safety issues.

If a battery gets swollen or puffy, do not use it. This is a sign the battery is damaged and could be dangerous. Contact DJI support if this happens.

Always store batteries in a cool, dry place when you're not using them. If you won't be flying for more than a few weeks, charge each battery to about 50% and store it in a cool location.

Propeller Safety and Storage

The propellers on the DJI Mini 5 Pro are sharp, and they can cause injury. Always handle them carefully.

When storing propellers, keep them in a safe place where children cannot access them. If a propeller is cracked or bent, do not use it. Replace it with a new one.

Propellers come in two types: clockwise rotating propellers and counterclockwise rotating propellers. When you install them, they must match the motor. The propellers are color-coded to help you match them correctly. We'll go through proper installation in a later chapter.

The Gimbal Protector

The gimbal protector is one of the most important protective accessories for your drone. The gimbal and camera system are delicate and can be easily damaged if the drone is dropped or bumped.

When you're not flying, always keep the gimbal protector attached to the drone. The protector clips onto the drone's body in front of the camera system.

Before you power on the drone to fly, always remove the gimbal protector by pulling the tab at the bottom. If you try to fly with the gimbal protector attached, the camera will be blocked and you won't see anything on your screen.

Charging Equipment Overview

The cables and chargers in your kit are essential. Always use official DJI charging equipment or high-quality third-party equipment. Using poor-quality chargers can damage your batteries and equipment.

The USB-C cables in your kit can charge the batteries, the controller, and the drone itself. Keep at least one cable with your flying kit at all times.

If your kit includes a charging hub, use it. It's faster and more convenient than charging one battery at a time.

Chapter 2

Your First Unboxing & Pre-Flight Assembly

Step-by-Step Unboxing

What You Should Check, Inspecting for Damage

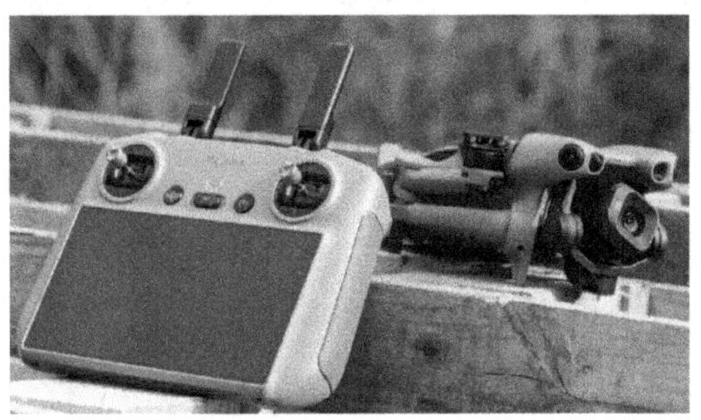

Unboxing your new drone is exciting, but it's also an important inspection process. Take your time and carefully check everything.

Find a clean, flat surface to work on—a table or desk is ideal. You'll need space to lay out all the components as you unbox them.

Open the main box carefully. The drone is the most delicate item, so DJI packs it very carefully. You'll see the drone in a protective carrying case at the top of the box.

Remove the carrying case and set it aside. Underneath, you'll find compartments containing the controller, batteries, charging hub (if you have the Fly More Kit), cables, spare propellers, and documentation.

As you remove each item from the box, place it on the table and inspect it visually. Look for:

Cracks or breaks in plastic components.

Dents or deformations in the body.

Loose connections or parts rattling inside.

Damaged packaging that suggests the item was dropped.

For the drone itself, open the protective carrying case and carefully lift the drone out. Inspect all sides:

Check the camera lens for cracks or scratches. The lens should be clear glass.

Look at the gimbal area. There should be no bent metal or misaligned components.

Check all four arms. They should be intact with no cracks.

Inspect the motors and propeller attachment points. They should look clean and undamaged.

Check the battery compartment on the bottom. It should be free of dents or cracks.

Look at the landing feet. All four should be present and uncracked.

For the controller, inspect the touchscreen for cracks, the buttons for damage, and the overall body for dents.

For the batteries, check the LED indicator lights. They should be intact and responsive when you press the button.

If you find any damage, do not attempt to use the equipment. Contact the retailer or DJI support immediately with photos of the damage for a replacement or refund.

If everything looks good, you're ready to proceed with assembly.

Removing Protective Film

Gimbal Protector, Lens Caps, Transport Covers

Before assembling, you need to remove several protective items that keep the drone safe during shipping.

The gimbal protector is the most important. It's a curved plastic cover on the front of the drone protecting the camera. This protector was necessary during shipping but must be removed before any operation of the drone.

Locate the small tab or pull handle at the bottom of the gimbal protector. Gently grip this tab and pull downward and backward. The protector will slide off. Set it aside in a safe place—you'll reattach it when storing the drone.

Some drones may have a lens cap (a small plastic cap covering the camera lens). If present, gently remove this cap by pulling it straight off.

Check the gimbal area for any protective film or stickers. Sometimes protective plastic sheets are applied to the gimbal for shipping. If you see plastic film, carefully peel it away.

Look at all the sensors (forward, backward, and downward) for protective covers. Remove any plastic covers protecting the sensor lenses.

Check the landing feet. Sometimes protective caps or stickers are applied. Remove any of these.

After removing all protective items, visually inspect the exposed areas. The gimbal should look like polished metal, the sensors should have clear lenses, and the landing feet should be ready to make contact with the ground.

Attaching Propellers

Proper Installation for Each Motor, The Color-Coding System

Now you'll attach the four propellers. This is critical—improper propeller installation can cause them to come loose during flight.

Lay out all four propellers on your work surface. Look at the markings on the blades:

Propellers with a single line, dot, or one color marking are clockwise (CW) rotating propellers.

Propellers with two lines, two dots, or different color marking are counterclockwise (CCW) rotating propellers.

You'll need two clockwise and two counterclockwise propellers.

Identify which propeller goes where:

Front-left motor: Clockwise propeller (single marking)

Front-right motor: Counterclockwise propeller (double marking)

Rear-left motor: Counterclockwise propeller (double marking)

Rear-right motor: Clockwise propeller (single marking)

This alternating pattern creates balanced thrust.

For the front-left motor:

Hold the drone steady and level.

Take a clockwise propeller and position it above the front-left motor shaft. The propeller has a center hole and a key or notch that aligns with the motor shaft. Orient the propeller to align with the shaft.

Push the propeller straight down onto the shaft with steady pressure. Do not use excessive force.

Continue pushing until you hear and feel a distinct click. This click is the locking mechanism engaging. The click is essential—it means the propeller is fully seated and locked.

Gently tug on the propeller to verify it's locked. It should not move, wiggle, or come off.

Repeat this process for the front-right motor with a counterclockwise propeller, rear-left with counterclockwise, and rear-right with clockwise.

Once all four propellers are installed, manually spin each one by hand. They should rotate smoothly and freely. If any feels stiff or grinds, remove it and reinstall it.

Installing Batteries

Where the Battery Slot Is, How It Clicks In, How to Remove It Safely

The battery compartment is on the bottom of the drone. You'll find a rectangular slot with electrical contacts inside.

Take a fully charged battery. The battery is a rectangular pack with four LED lights on one end (the end with the metal contacts).

Look at the battery slot on the drone bottom. The slot has a specific shape—the battery will only fit one way.

Orient the battery so the metal contacts (the end with the LED lights) face into the slot. This is the bottom end of the battery.

Align the battery with the slot opening. The edges should align with the slot guides.

Gently push the battery straight into the slot. You're not forcing—just steady, straight pressure.

Push until you feel the battery click and lock into place. You should hear and feel a definite click. The click means the battery is fully inserted and locked.

The battery should not wiggle, move around, or come loose. Test by gently tugging on the battery. It should be firmly attached.

To remove the battery safely:

On each side of the battery, there are small release buttons or tabs.

Press both release buttons simultaneously while gently pulling the battery straight out.

The battery will disengage and slide out. Don't yank or twist—pull straight out.

Once removed, set the battery aside safely.

Control Stick Installation

Where They Slot, Which Direction They Go, Ensuring They Click Fully

The two control sticks attach to the bottom of the controller. If they're not already installed, you'll need to install them before flying.

Look at the bottom of the controller. You'll see two small recessed sockets, one on the left side and one on the right side. These are where the sticks go.

Take the left control stick. The bottom end has a connector with a specific shape (usually a plus-sign or cross shape). This connector is designed to fit only one way into the socket.

Hold the stick vertically, with the connector facing downward.

Align the connector with the left socket opening on the controller bottom.

Gently push the stick straight down into the socket. You're not forcing hard—just steady, straight pressure.

Push until you hear and feel a click. The click indicates the stick is fully seated and locked in place. This click is important.

Test the left stick by gently moving it in all directions. It should move smoothly and return to center when released. It should not wiggle on the controller or feel loose.

Repeat the same process for the right control stick and right socket.

After both sticks are installed, test them together. Move the left stick up and down and side to side. Move the right stick in all directions. Both should move smoothly without any grinding, sticking, or resistance.

Unfolding the Drone

Proper Sequence (Front Arms, Rear Arms), Listening for Click Sounds

With the battery and propellers installed, you're ready to unfold the drone for flight.

Hold the drone with the body level and horizontal. The arms are currently folded flat against the sides of the body.

Start with the front arms. Grab the front-left arm near where it connects to the body. Pull it outward and away from the body. Pull steadily until the arm is perpendicular to the body (at a 90-degree angle).

As you reach the extended position, you should hear and feel a click. This click is the arm locking mechanism engaging. The click confirms the arm is fully extended and locked.

The front-left arm should now be in the flight position and should not fold back inward if you gently push on it.

Repeat for the front-right arm. Pull it outward until perpendicular, listen for the click, and confirm it's locked.

Now move to the rear arms. Grab the rear-left arm and pull it outward. Pull until it's perpendicular to the body and you hear the click.

Finally, unfold the rear-right arm the same way.

Important: When you unfold the rear-right arm and fully lock it, the drone may automatically power on. This is the "auto power-on" feature. Be ready when this happens. The drone will beep and start its self-diagnostic sequence.

After all four arms are unfolded and locked, visually verify:

All four arms are fully extended perpendicular to the body.

All four propellers are pointing upward, not folded down.

No arms are in an intermediate or partially folded position.

The drone should look like a plus sign or cross shape when viewed from above.

Powering On Sequence

What Happens First, How Long to Wait for Self-Diagnostics

Once the drone is fully assembled, you're ready to power on the system.

The correct sequence is: Controller first, then Drone.

Power on the remote controller:

Locate the power button on the back center of the controller.

Press the power button once (a single quick press).

Immediately press and hold the same button for about two seconds until you hear a beep.

The controller will power up and its LED lights will illuminate.

The controller screen will take a moment to display.

Wait until the controller screen is fully active and showing the home screen or app launcher. This usually takes 10-15 seconds.

Once the controller is ready, power on the drone:

Locate the power button on the top back area of the drone.

Press the power button once (a single quick press).

Immediately press and hold the same button for about two seconds until you hear a beep from the drone.

The drone will power up.

During power-up, the drone's self-diagnostic system activates:

You'll hear brief motor spinning sounds as the system tests each motor. This is normal.

The gimbal will move slightly as the system tests gimbal operation. This is normal.

Various LED lights on the drone will blink in patterns as the system runs diagnostics. This is normal.

Do not be alarmed by these sounds and movements. They are expected and indicate the system is functioning properly.

The self-diagnostic sequence takes approximately 30 to 60 seconds. During this time:

Hold the drone steady in your hands. Don't set it down yet.

Do not move the control sticks.

Wait patiently for the diagnostics to complete.

After the self-diagnostics complete, the drone will settle into a quiet, hovering-ready state. The propellers will stop spinning. The gimbal will stop moving. The system will be waiting for your input.

On the controller screen, you should see the live camera feed from the drone. This indicates successful connection between the controller and drone.

The status LED on the back of the controller should be green (indicating a good connection).

If the status LED is red or blinking, there's a connection problem. Do not proceed with flying. Power off and troubleshoot.

Visual Inspection before First Flight

Propeller Check, Arm Security, Gimbal Movement, Sensor Check

Before your first actual flight, perform this final visual and physical inspection.

Propeller check: Walk around the drone and examine all four propellers. Look for any cracks, bends, or damage that weren't visible before. Manually spin each propeller by hand—it should rotate smoothly. Check that each propeller is fully clicked in and doesn't wiggle on the shaft.

Arm security: Visually verify that all four arms are fully extended. Gently push on each arm to confirm it doesn't fold back. The arms should be rigid and locked in place. There should be no flexibility or looseness in the arm connections.

Gimbal movement: While holding the drone, use the left dial on the controller to tilt the gimbal up and down. The camera should move smoothly and respond immediately to your input. Move it up (toward the sky), to center (straight ahead), and down (toward the ground). The movement should be smooth without grinding sounds.

Camera lens inspection: Look directly at the camera lens on the front of the drone. The lens should be clean and clear with no dust, fingerprints, or protective covers. If the lens is dirty, gently clean it with a microfiber cloth before flying.

Landing feet check: Flip the drone over (if you have someone to help, or carefully flip it yourself) and visually inspect all four landing feet. They should all be present, intact, and not cracked.

Sensor visual check: Look at the forward-facing cameras on the front of the drone (below the main camera). They should be visible and unobstructed. Look at the downward-facing cameras on the bottom of the drone. They should be visible. Look for the LiDAR sensor (a small opening on the bottom). It should be clean.

Battery secure check: Check that the battery is fully inserted and locked in the battery compartment. Gently tug on the battery to confirm it won't come loose.

Control stick test: While holding the drone, move both control sticks through their full range of motion. They should move smoothly and return to center automatically when released.

If everything passes this inspection, you're ready for your first hover test.

If you find any issues or damage, do not fly. Address the issue first. Safety is paramount.

Important Reminders for First Assembly and Flight

Never fly with the gimbal protector attached. The camera will be blocked.

Never fly with the protective film still on sensors or lenses.

Always verify propellers are fully clicked in—this is critical for safety.

Always wait for the self-diagnostic sequence to complete before attempting to fly.

Always perform the pre-flight visual inspection.

Never fly if any component looks damaged or questionable.

Always fly in an open area away from people, animals, and obstacles during your first flights.

Chapter 3

The DJI Fly App - Getting Started

Downloading & Installing

Where to Get It (App Store, Google Play), System Requirements

The DJI Fly app is the control center for your drone. It's how you see what the camera sees, control the drone, and configure settings. You must download and install this app before your first flight.

The app is available for both iOS and Android devices. It's free to download and use.

For iPhone or iPad users:

Open the App Store on your Apple device.

Tap the search icon at the bottom of the screen.

Type "DJI Fly" in the search box.

Look for the official DJI Fly app (the icon shows a stylized drone silhouette). It should have "DJI" as the developer name.

Tap "Get" to download the app.

You may be prompted to authenticate using Face ID, Touch ID, or your Apple password. Complete the authentication.

Wait for the download and installation to complete. This usually takes 1-2 minutes depending on internet speed.

Once installed, the "Get" button will change to "Open." Tap to launch the app for the first time.

For Android users:

Open Google Play Store on your Android device.

Tap the search icon at the bottom (magnifying glass).

Type "DJI Fly" in the search box.

Look for the official DJI Fly app (developed by DJI). The icon should show a drone silhouette.

Tap "Install" to download the app.

Google Play may ask for permission to access certain device features. Approve these permissions.

Wait for installation to complete. This usually takes 1-2 minutes.

Once installed, the "Install" button will change to "Open." Tap to launch the app for the first time.

System requirements:

For iOS: iPhone or iPad running iOS 14.0 or later. A device from the last 5-7 years will work fine.

For Android: An Android device running Android 9.0 or later. Most modern Android phones will work. Some older budget phones may not meet requirements.

Internet connection: You need a stable internet connection to download the app and log in. After login, you can use the app without internet once connected to your controller, but you need internet for initial setup.

Screen size: A larger screen is more comfortable for flying. A phone is adequate; a tablet is even better.

Storage space: The app requires about 500 MB of free storage space on your device.

Creating Your DJI Account

Why You Need One, Two-Factor Authentication, DJI Care Refresh

When you first launch the DJI Fly app, you'll be prompted to create or log in to a DJI account. This is a mandatory step.

Why you need a DJI account:

It registers your drone to you. This is essential for activating your drone and for support purposes.

It tracks your flight records and flight history.

It enables DJI Care Refresh, which is DJI's insurance/protection plan for your drone.

It allows you to synchronize settings and preferences across multiple devices.

It gives you access to DJI's online services and updates.

Creating a new DJI account (if you don't have one):

On the login screen, look for an option like "Create Account" or "Sign Up."

You'll be asked to provide:

An email address (this becomes your account username)

A strong password (at least 8 characters, mix of uppercase, lowercase, numbers, and symbols)

Your first and last name

After entering this information, DJI will send a verification email to your email address. Check your email and click the verification link.

Once verified, your account is created.

Two-factor authentication (2FA):

Two-factor authentication is a security feature that adds an extra layer of protection to your account. When enabled, login attempts require not just your password, but also a verification code sent to your phone or email.

To enable two-factor authentication:

Log in to your DJI account.

Go to Account Settings or Security Settings.

Look for "Two-Factor Authentication" or "2FA."

Enable it.

Choose your delivery method: SMS (text message to your phone) or email.

DJI will send a verification code to your chosen method.

Enter the code to confirm and enable 2FA.

Once enabled, every time you log in from a new device, you'll need to enter the verification code. This makes your account very secure.

Important: Write down your account recovery codes if DJI provides them. These are backup codes that let you recover your account if you lose access to your phone or email.

DJI Care Refresh:

DJI Care Refresh is an optional insurance and protection plan for your drone. It's not required, but it's highly recommended for beginners.

What DJI Care Refresh covers:

Accidental damage (like a crash into a tree or building)

Water damage (if you accidentally fly near water and it gets wet)

Motor/propeller failures

Battery failures

Gimbal or camera damage

What DJI Care Refresh does NOT cover:

Deliberate damage or abuse

Flying in unsafe conditions

Loss or theft of the drone

Pre-existing damage not reported

How DJI Care Refresh works:

You pay an upfront fee (varies by region, typically $50-100 USD for the Mini 5 Pro).

This covers 2 years of protection.

If your drone is damaged, you can file a claim.

DJI will either repair or replace your drone for a reduced fee (usually $95-150 per incident).

You get 2 claim incidents during the 2-year period.

To purchase DJI Care Refresh:

When you first access your account in the app, DJI will prompt you to purchase DJI Care Refresh.

You can also go to Account Settings > DJI Care Refresh to purchase it later.

Follow the on-screen prompts to complete the purchase.

Your DJI Care Refresh coverage will be immediately active.

For a beginner, DJI Care Refresh is highly recommended because crashes happen while learning. The peace of mind is worth the cost.

Activating Your Drone

What This Means, Why It's Required, Firmware Update Process

Activation is a one-time process where you register your drone to your DJI account. This is required before you can fly.

What activation does:

It links your drone's serial number to your DJI account.

It records ownership information in DJI's database.

It ensures you're the legal owner and operator.

It may enable certain features or services.

Why it's required:

It's DJI's way of preventing stolen drones from being used.

It's required by law in some countries for regulatory compliance.

It enables warranty service and support.

How to activate your drone:

Once you log in to the DJI Fly app, the app will prompt you to activate your drone the first time you connect to the controller.

The activation process is simple: the app will ask you to confirm you're the owner by entering your account password.

You may be asked to agree to terms and conditions.

Once confirmed, activation is complete. This usually takes less than a minute.

Important: Activation requires an internet connection. If your device doesn't have internet when you try to activate, you'll need to move to a location with Wi-Fi or cellular signal.

Firmware update process:

Firmware is the software running on your drone and controller. DJI regularly releases firmware updates that fix bugs, add features, and improve safety.

When you first activate your drone, the app will check if there are any available firmware updates.

If updates are available, the app will prompt you to install them. You'll see a message like "New Firmware Available."

The app will show:

What version you currently have

What version is available

What improvements are included in the update

You have the option to update now or skip.

For your first flight, it's highly recommended to update immediately. New firmware often includes important safety improvements and bug fixes.

To update firmware:

Ensure your drone and controller batteries are fully charged (crucial—a firmware update cannot be interrupted by low battery).

Keep your device connected to Wi-Fi for a stable internet connection.

Tap "Update" when prompted.

The app will download the firmware update (this may take 5-10 minutes depending on file size and internet speed).

Once downloaded, the update process will begin. You'll see progress indicators.

The drone will briefly power cycle during the update. This is normal.

The controller will also update separately.

Do not power off, disconnect, or move away during the update.

The entire update process typically takes 15-30 minutes.

Once complete, the app will notify you that the update was successful.

Never interrupt a firmware update. Always ensure full battery charge before starting.

First App Launch

Permissions Needed (Location, Camera, Bluetooth), Connecting to Controller

When you first launch the DJI Fly app, the system will ask for various permissions. These are necessary for the app to function properly.

Permissions you'll be asked to grant:

Location permission: The app needs to know your location for geofencing (preventing flight in restricted airspace), flight records, and map features. You should grant "Allow All the Time" or "Allow While Using App." Location permission is essential.

Camera permission: The app needs camera access to display the live feed from your drone's camera on your screen. Without this permission, you can't see what the drone sees. Grant this permission.

Bluetooth permission: The app needs Bluetooth to connect to your remote controller wirelessly. This is essential for controlling the drone. Grant this permission.

Microphone permission: Some features (like recording audio during video flight) may request microphone permission. This is optional but recommended.

Photo library or storage access: The app may ask to access your device's photo library to save photos and videos. Grant this permission.

To grant permissions on iOS:

When the app prompts for a permission, a dialog will appear asking "Allow DJI Fly to access [permission]?"

Tap "Allow" to grant the permission.

If you deny a permission by mistake, go to Settings > DJI Fly and manually enable the permission.

To grant permissions on Android:

When the app prompts, a dialog appears asking for permission.

Tap "Allow" or "Allow All the Time" depending on the permission.

If you deny by mistake, go to Settings > Apps > DJI Fly > Permissions and enable it.

Connecting to the controller for the first time:

Once permissions are granted, the app will prompt you to connect to your remote controller.

Ensure your controller is powered on (press and hold the power button until you hear a beep).

On the app's connection screen, it will show "Looking for Controller" or "Searching for Device."

The app will scan for your controller via Bluetooth.

Your controller's name will appear (usually "DJI RC-N1" or similar for the RC 2).

Tap on your controller's name to pair.

You may see a pairing confirmation dialog. Confirm the pairing.

Once paired, the app will show "Connected" next to your controller's name.

The app will then attempt to connect to your drone (if powered on).

Once the drone is connected, you'll see the live camera feed on the screen.

If connection fails:

Ensure the controller is powered on.

Ensure Bluetooth is enabled on your device.

Restart the app and try connecting again.

Power off the controller, wait 10 seconds, power it back on, and try again.

Check if another device is connected to the controller and disconnect it first.

The Main Screen Layout

Camera View, Home Icon, Settings, Menu Locations

Once you're connected and ready to fly, you'll see the main flight screen. Understanding the layout is crucial for safe flying.

The main flight screen has several zones:

Center of screen: The live camera feed from the drone. This is what the drone's camera is seeing in real-time. This is the most important visual reference during flight.

Top-left corner: Home icon (usually marked with an "H" or house symbol). Tapping this returns you to the home screen and any menu.

Top-right corner: Settings icon (usually a gear symbol). Tapping this accesses flight settings and adjustments.

Center-bottom of screen: Record/Shutter button (large red circle). Tap to take a photo or start/stop video recording. The color may change when recording.

Bottom-left: Pause button (two vertical bars). Tap to pause the drone's current movement and hold position.

Bottom-right: Return to Home (RTH) button (usually marked with an up arrow). Tap to make the drone automatically return to its takeoff location.

Left side panel (appears during flight): Shows battery percentage, signal strength, gimbal status, flight mode, and camera settings. Swipe this panel to access more information.

Right side panel (appears during flight): Shows altitude (height above ground), distance from home, current speed, GPS status, and estimated flight time remaining. Swipe this panel to see more details.

Status bar (usually top of screen): Displays overall system status, time, signal indicator, and connection status.

The layout adapts slightly depending on whether you're on the home screen, in pre-flight setup, or actively flying. However, the basic zones remain consistent.

Navigating Between Screens

The Back Button, How to Return to Home Screen

Navigation in the DJI Fly app is straightforward but important to understand.

The home icon (top-left corner):

Tapping the home icon from any screen (flight screen, settings, or menus) returns you to the main home screen.

On the home screen, you see options like "Start Flight," "Gallery," "Settings," and "More."

From the home screen, you can access any part of the app.

The back button:

Most screens have a back button, usually at the top-left or accessible by swiping from the left edge.

On Android, the system back button (the arrow at the bottom) also works to navigate back in the app.

Tapping back returns you to the previous screen you were on.

Repeatedly tapping back will eventually return you to the home screen.

Never use force-close or swipe-away on the app. Always use the proper navigation buttons. Force-closing the app during a flight or critical operation can cause unexpected behavior.

Returning to the home screen from flight mode:

If you're actively flying and want to return to the home screen, tap the pause button to pause the drone first.

Then tap the home icon.

The app will show a warning asking if you want to leave flight mode. Confirm that you want to exit.

The drone will enter Attitude Mode (ready to be controlled manually) or auto-hover depending on your settings.

Once safely hovering, you can return to the home screen.

Screen Controls in Flight Mode

Where to Tap for Each Function, Full-Screen vs Split-Screen

During actual flight, the app has additional controls and display modes.

Record/Shutter button (center-bottom):

For photos: Tap once to capture a single photo. The camera will focus and take the shot.

For video: Tap and hold to start recording. Tap again to stop recording. During recording, the button usually glows red or changes appearance to indicate active recording.

You can also use the recording button on the physical controller to control the camera while flying.

Gimbal tilt control (left panel):

Swipe up and down on the left panel to tilt the camera up and down.

Or use the physical left dial on the controller.

Zoom control (right panel):

Swipe left and right on the right panel to zoom in or out (1x, 2x, 4x).

Or use the physical right dial on the controller.

Full-screen vs split-screen mode:

The app can display in full-screen flight view (only the live camera feed) or split-screen (camera feed plus information panels on sides).

To toggle between modes: Pinch inward (two-finger squeeze) on the screen or look for a display mode button (usually near the home icon).

Full-screen mode: Maximizes the camera view, giving you a better look at what you're shooting. Useful for precise framing and composition.

Split-screen mode: Displays the camera feed alongside flight information (altitude, distance, battery, speed). More information at a glance, but less screen space for the camera view.

Swipe gestures during flight:

Swipe from left edge inward: Shows left panel with battery, signal, and camera info.

Swipe from right edge inward: Shows right panel with altitude, distance, and flight info.

Swipe down from top: May show additional status information depending on app version.

Pinch on screen: Zoom in/out (in some modes) or toggle full/split screen.

Flight information overlay:

Altitude: Your current height above ground (meters or feet depending on settings).

Distance: Your distance from the home point (takeoff location).

Speed: Your current velocity in meters per second or kilometers per hour.

GPS status: Number of GPS satellites connected (usually 10+ is good).

Battery: Percentage remaining and estimated flight time.

Signal: Strength of the connection between controller and drone.

You can customize which information displays on the screen through settings.

Troubleshooting Connection Issues

What to Do If Controller Won't Connect, App Crashes

Connection problems are the most common issue beginners face. Here's how to troubleshoot.

Controller won't connect to app:

Check that the controller is powered on (you should hear a beep and see LED lights).

Check that Bluetooth is enabled on your device (go to Settings > Bluetooth and turn it on if off).

Check that the controller isn't already paired to another device. If it is, disconnect it from that device first.

Restart the controller: Power it off, wait 10 seconds, power it back on.

Restart your device: Power off your phone or tablet, wait 10 seconds, power it back on.

Restart the app: Completely close the DJI Fly app. Go to your device's settings and "Force Stop" the app. Then reopen it.

Update the app: Go to your device's app store and check if there's a newer version of the DJI Fly app. Update if available.

If none of these work, try pairing again: Go to your device's Bluetooth settings, "Forget" the controller device, then in the DJI Fly app, tap "Scan" or "Connect" to pair again from scratch.

Drone won't connect to controller/app:

Ensure the drone is powered on (you should hear beeps and see LED lights blinking).

Ensure the controller is powered on and connected to the app first.

Check that the drone and controller are within Bluetooth range (usually 100 meters in open space).

Check that the drone's antennas are vertical and unfolded. Folded or bent antennas prevent signal transmission.

Restart the drone: Power it off, wait 10 seconds, power it back on.

If the drone still won't connect, perform a controller and drone "pairing reset": Go to Settings > Control > Pairing Reset. Follow the on-screen instructions to re-pair the controller to the drone from scratch.

App crashes or freezes during flight:

If the app crashes while you're flying, the drone will not immediately fall. The drone will enter a safe hold mode and hover in place.

Take a moment to restart the app: Close it and reopen it.

Once reconnected, check the drone's current status on the screen.

If the drone appears safe (hovering in place, not drifting), you can resume control carefully.

If the app repeatedly crashes during flight, land the drone immediately and troubleshoot before flying again.

To prevent crashes:

Keep the app updated to the latest version.

Ensure your device has sufficient free storage space (at least 1-2 GB).

Close other apps running in the background to free up memory.

Avoid flying in areas with strong wireless interference (like near powerful radio transmitters or in urban areas with dense cellular networks).

Ensure your device's operating system is up to date.

Connection drops during flight (app shows "Disconnected" but drone continues):

If the app loses connection to the drone momentarily, the drone will continue flying based on its last received instructions.

The drone will auto-hover if it loses signal for more than a few seconds.

Try to re-establish connection by moving closer to the drone or moving to a location with less interference.

If connection is repeatedly lost, land immediately and troubleshoot.

Possible causes of repeated disconnections:

Weak signal due to distance or obstacles.

Electromagnetic interference in the area.

Controller or drone firmware out of date.

Damaged or misaligned antennas on the controller.

Chapter 4

The RC 2 Remote Controller - Physical Tour

Controller Layout from Top View

What You See When Holding It

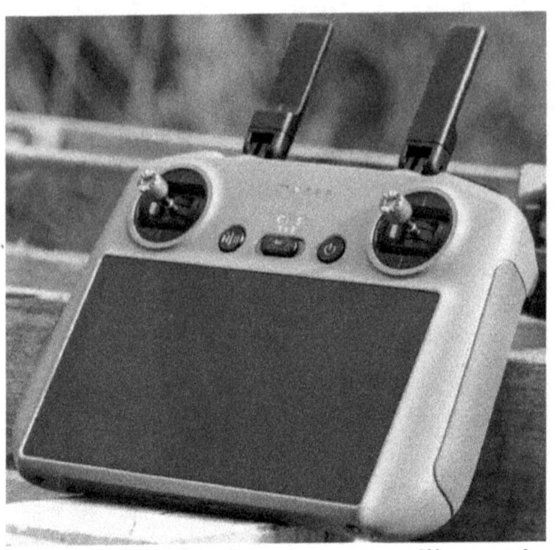

When you hold the DJI RC 2 controller in both hands, you're looking at what pilots call the "top view." This is the perspective you'll have during flight. Understanding what you're looking at will help you control the drone effectively.

The most prominent feature is the touchscreen at the top of the controller. This is where you'll see the live camera feed from your drone. The screen shows what the drone's camera is seeing in real-time. The screen is also where you interact with the DJI Fly app to access menus, settings, and flight information.

Below the screen, on the left side, is the left control stick. This stick is mounted in a recessed area and moves up and down and side to side. Your left hand holds this side of the controller, and your thumb controls this stick.

On the right side is the right control stick. Like the left one, it moves in all directions. Your right hand holds this side and operates this stick with your thumb.

Between the two control sticks, closer to your body, is the left dial. This is a rotating wheel above the left control stick. You rotate it with your left hand to control the gimbal tilt (camera angle up and down).

On the right side, in a similar position, is the right dial. This dial controls zoom. You rotate it with your right hand to zoom in or out.

On the top-right area of the controller, you'll see two buttons. The upper button is the focus/shutter button. The lower button is the record button. These buttons are used for taking photos and recording videos.

At the very top of the controller, you'll see two small antenna stubs standing upright. These antennas send and receive signals with the drone. They should always be vertical when flying.

Controller Layout from Bottom View

The Customizable Buttons Underneath

If you flip the controller upside down (without powering it on), you're looking at the "bottom view." This is where some important buttons are located.

The most notable features on the bottom are the left handle and right handle. These curved sections are where your hands naturally grip when flying. They're part of the controller's body and provide comfortable grip points.

On the bottom-left side of the controller, near your left hand, is the C1 button. This is a customizable button. Its primary function can be changed through the DJI Fly app settings.

On the bottom-right side, near your right hand, is the C2 button. Like C1, this is customizable and its function depends on how you configure it in the app.

In the center of the bottom, you'll see the USB-C charging port. This is where you plug in the charging cable to charge the controller's battery. It's also used for data transfer if needed.

Next to the USB-C port, you'll see the microSD card slot. This is a small rectangular opening where you can insert a microSD memory card. The card stores video recordings and photos from the controller's screen.

Near the center of the bottom-back area is the Return to Home (RTH) button. This large, slightly recessed button tells the drone to return to its takeoff point. It's positioned for easy thumb access during flight.

The Power Button

Where It Is, How to Press It

The power button is located on the back of the controller, in the center area. You'll find it if you turn the controller to face you with the screen toward your face. The power button is a small, recessed button. It's not a large, obvious button—it's subtle by design to prevent accidental presses. The power button serves multiple functions depending on how you press it.

To check the battery level, press the power button once. A single quick press. When you do this, the LED lights on the back of the controller will briefly light up to show you the battery status. This is useful when the controller is already powered off, and you want to see if it has enough charge.

To power on the controller, press the power button once (single press), and then immediately press and hold the same button for about two seconds. Keep holding even after you hear the beep sound. The controller will power on and be ready to communicate with the drone. You should hear a confirmation beep when it's fully powered on.

To power off the controller, use the same sequence: press once, then press and hold for about two seconds until you hear a beep. This beep confirms that the controller is shutting down. Release the button after the beep.

Important: Do not rapidly press the button multiple times. A single press followed by a hold is the correct technique.

The Control Sticks

Where They Go, How They Slot In, How They Control the Drone

The two control sticks are the primary way you control the drone's movement during flight. Each stick can move in four directions: up, down, left, and right.

The left control stick is mounted below the left side of the screen. When the controller is assembled, the stick stands vertically from the controller's body. To install the left stick if it's not already attached, take the stick and look at the connector on its bottom end. The connector has a specific shape designed to fit only one way into the socket on the controller.

Hold the stick vertically above the left socket on the controller. Align the connector with the socket opening. Gently push the stick straight down until it clicks into place. You should feel the stick lock in. The click is important—it means the stick is fully seated and secure. If the stick feels loose or doesn't click, remove it and try again.

To test if it's properly installed, gently tug on the stick. It should not come loose. It should feel firmly attached. Gently move the stick in all directions. It should move smoothly in every direction and return to the center position when you release it.

The right control stick is installed the same way on the right side of the controller. Use the same sequence: hold it vertically, align the connector, push down until you feel the click, and test it for smooth movement.

During flight, the left control stick controls two things:

Moving the stick up makes the drone rise (ascend). Moving it down makes the drone descend (go down). These are the vertical movements.

Moving the stick left rotates the drone counterclockwise (spins left). Moving the stick right rotates the drone clockwise (spins right). These movements rotate the entire drone while keeping it in the same location.

The right control stick also controls two things:

Moving the stick forward makes the drone move forward (away from you). Moving the stick backward makes the drone move backward (toward you). These are forward and backward movements.

Moving the stick left makes the drone move left (strafe left). Moving the stick right makes the drone move right (strafe right). These are sideways movements without rotating the drone.

Important: The control sticks should move smoothly and return to the center automatically when you release them. If a stick feels stiff, grinds, or doesn't return to center, do not fly. There's likely a problem that needs attention.

The Dials Explained

Left Dial (Gimbal Tilt), Right Dial (Zoom), What They Do in Flight

The dials are rotating wheels on the controller. Unlike the control sticks, they rotate rather than move in four directions.

The left dial is positioned above and slightly to the left of the left control stick. You operate it with your left hand, usually your left hand's fingers (not your thumb, which is on the stick).

The left dial controls gimbal tilt, which is the vertical angle of the camera. Rotating the dial forward (toward the top of the controller) tilts the camera upward so it points toward the sky. Rotating the dial backward (toward the bottom of the controller) tilts the camera downward so it points toward the ground.

The gimbal has a range. It can tilt upward to about 25 degrees (slightly above horizontal) and downward to 90 degrees (straight down). This range allows you to capture images and video from many different angles without moving the drone itself.

During a flight, you might tilt the camera up to show the landscape ahead of you while flying forward. Or you might tilt it straight down to see the ground beneath the drone. You can also return it to horizontal (pointing straight ahead) by rotating the dial back to its middle position.

The right dial is positioned above and slightly to the right of the right control stick. You operate it with your right hand, usually your right hand's fingers.

The right dial controls zoom. Zoom allows you to make distant objects appear closer without the drone moving. The Mini 5 Pro has three zoom levels: 1x (normal, native view), 2x (medium zoom), and 4x (digital zoom with some quality loss).

Rotating the dial forward (toward the top) zooms in, making things appear larger and closer. Rotating the dial backward (toward the bottom) zooms out, making things appear smaller and farther away.

The zoom is useful when you want to frame a distant subject, look at details of a far-away building, or create a dramatic effect by zooming in on something specific. The 2x zoom on the Mini 5 Pro is especially useful because it maintains good quality compared to the 4x digital zoom.

The Five Key Buttons on Top:

Recording Button, Focus/Shutter Button, and What Each Does

On the top-right area of the controller, you'll find the most important buttons for actually taking photos and recording videos.

The focus/shutter button is the upper button. This button has a specific function:

Pressing it halfway down (not all the way) triggers autofocus. This tells the camera to focus on a subject. The drone's autofocus system analyzes the image and locks onto what it thinks is the subject. This is useful when you want to ensure a specific subject is sharp before taking a photo.

Pressing it all the way down takes a still photo. The camera captures a single image and saves it. This is how you take photos with your drone.

The record button is the lower button, positioned just below the focus/shutter button. This button starts and stops video recording.

Pressing it once starts recording video. The camera begins capturing video to the microSD card or internal storage. A red indicator light usually illuminates when recording is active, so you know the camera is capturing footage.

Pressing it again stops recording. The video file is saved automatically.

One important note: if you press and hold the record button (rather than just pressing once), it might switch the camera between photo and video mode. This changes what the camera will do when you press the shutter button. Usually, you'll tap the mode selector on the screen instead to change between photo and video modes, so avoid holding the record button unless you're intentionally switching modes.

LED Indicators:

What the Colored Lights Mean (Battery, Connection Status)

The LED lights on the controller provide important information at a glance without needing to look at the screen.

The status LED is located on the back of the controller. This small light indicates the connection status between the controller and the drone.
When the status LED is green (or solid), it means the controller and drone are properly connected and ready to fly. This is the status you want to see before flying.
When the status LED is red or blinking, it means there's a connection problem. The drone and controller cannot communicate. Do not try to fly. Power off everything and check for issues.
When the status LED is amber or yellow, it might indicate a warning condition. Check the DJI Fly app on the screen for specific error messages.
The battery level LEDs are located on the back of the controller. These are usually a series of small lights arranged like a battery indicator (similar to what you see on a phone).
When all the lights are on, the controller battery is fully charged (100%).
When most of the lights are on, the battery has good charge (75-99%).
When about half the lights are on, the battery is at about 50% charge.
When only one or two lights are on, the battery is low (below 25%). You should charge the controller soon.
When no lights are on, the battery is empty or critically low.
To check the battery level at any time, press the power button once. The battery LED lights will briefly illuminate to show the current charge level.

USB-C Charging Port & microSD Slot

Where to Charge, How to Insert Memory Card

The USB-C charging port is located on the bottom of the controller. This small rectangular port is where you connect a USB-C charging cable to charge the controller's battery.

To charge the controller, plug a USB-C cable into the port. The other end of the cable connects to a power adapter (usually a 5V or 9V USB power adapter) that plugs into wall power.

When you plug the cable in, you should see an LED light indicate that charging has started. The light behavior depends on the current charge level. Full charging usually takes about 1.5 to 2 hours with a standard power adapter.

Do not charge the controller when it's powered on. Power it off first, then plug in the charging cable.

The microSD card slot is next to the USB-C port on the bottom of the controller. This slot holds a microSD memory card. MicroSD cards are small rectangular cards that store video, photos, and other data.

To insert a microSD card, locate the slot. It's a small rectangular opening on the bottom of the controller. The card is designed to fit only one way, so you won't be able to force it incorrectly.

Hold the microSD card with the label facing outward (the side you'd read text from). Align the card with the slot opening and gently push it straight in. The card will slide into the slot until it clicks. The click indicates the card is fully inserted and locked.

To remove the microSD card, push it straight in slightly. The card will disengage from the lock mechanism and pop out partially. You can then pull it out by hand.

The microSD card stores video recordings from the drone and screenshots you take of the controller screen. If you want to keep a record of what the controller screen showed during a flight, the microSD card is where that data is stored.

Not all flights require a microSD card—the drone's video is stored on the drone itself. However, many pilots use a microSD card as backup storage or to record the controller screen during flights.

Important Maintenance Tips for the Controller

Keep the controller's screen clean. Use a microfiber cloth to gently wipe the screen. Do not use harsh chemicals or rough materials.

Keep the buttons and dials clean. They should move smoothly. If they become sticky or sluggish, gently clean around them with a soft cloth.

Avoid exposing the controller to extreme heat or cold. Store it in a temperature-controlled environment.

Charge the controller fully before each flying session. An empty controller battery means you can't fly.

Do not drop the controller or expose it to water. It's not waterproof.

The antennas should always be vertical when flying. Folding them down during storage is fine, but unfold them before flight.

Chapter 5

Assembly and Pre-Flight Checks - Getting Your Drone Ready to Fly

Before You Begin

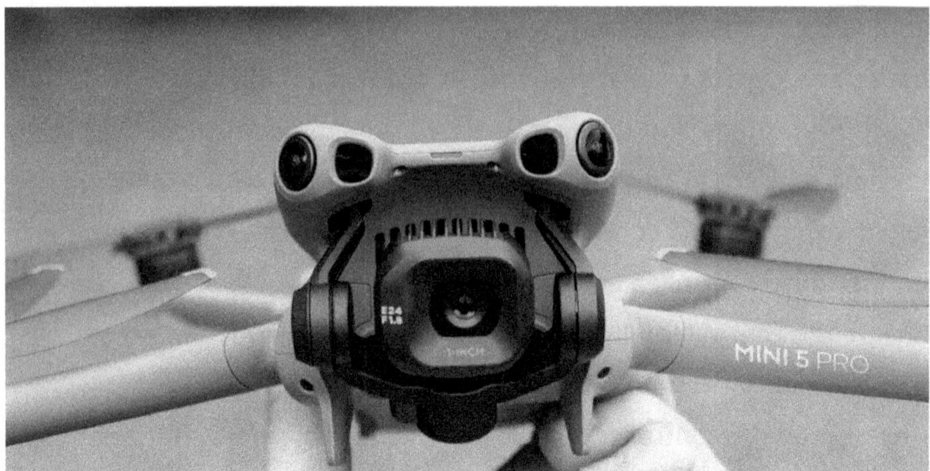

Before you start assembling your drone, find a clean, flat surface like a table or desk. You'll want space to lay out all the pieces and work comfortably. Make sure your hands are clean and dry.

Remove your drone from the box carefully. The drone is delicate, so handle it gently. Don't force anything—all connections are designed to fit smoothly.

Step 1: Remove the Gimbal Protector

The gimbal protector is the plastic cover on the front of the drone. This cover protects the camera and gimbal system during transport and storage.

Look at the front of the drone. You'll see the gimbal protector is a curved plastic piece. At the bottom of this protector, there's a small tab labeled "PULL."

Hold the drone with one hand, steady and level. With your other hand, grab the tab at the bottom of the gimbal protector and pull it downward and away from the drone. The protector will slide off cleanly.

The gimbal protector is not needed for flying, but you should keep it for when you transport the drone in the future. Set it aside in a safe place.

Important: Look at the front of the drone now. You should see the camera lens clearly. The camera looks like a small glass circle at the very front. If you don't see it clearly, the gimbal protector may not be fully removed. Check again.

Step 2: Attach the Four Propellers

The propellers are the spinning blades that make your drone fly. Each propeller clips onto one of the four motors at the end of each arm.

Your kit includes extra propellers, but you'll use four of them to fly. The propellers come in two types: clockwise-rotating (often marked with a single line or colored tape) and counterclockwise-rotating (often marked with two lines or different colored tape).

There are two propellers for the front of the drone and two for the back. The front propellers are identical to each other. The back propellers are identical to each other. But front and back propellers are different from each other.

Look at the four motors on the ends of the drone's arms. Each motor has a small clip or opening at its top.

Starting with the front-left motor (on the left side of the drone when you're looking at the camera):

Take a front-left propeller (the type marked for the front position). Hold it above the motor so the clip opening aligns with the small notch on the motor. Gently push the propeller down onto the motor until you hear or feel a click. The click means it's locked in place.

Repeat this for the front-right motor (on the right side at the front).

Now attach the back propellers. These are different from the front ones, so make sure you're using the correct type. Repeat the same clicking process for both rear motors.

All four propellers should now be attached and spinning freely when you gently flick them by hand. They should not wobble or come loose.

Check each propeller carefully. Look for any cracks, bends, or damage. If you see any damage, do not fly. Replace that propeller with a new one from your spare parts.

Step 3: Insert a Fully Charged Battery

The Intelligent Flight Battery is what powers your drone to fly. You should have at least one battery that's fully charged.

Turn the drone upside down so you can see the battery slot on the bottom. The slot is a rectangular opening with contacts on the inside.

Take your fully charged battery. The battery is a rectangular pack with LED lights on one end. The end with the contacts (the shiny metal part) goes into the slot.

Hold the battery and align it with the slot opening. The battery will only fit one way, so don't force it. Gently slide the battery into the slot and push it in until you hear a click. The click means the battery is locked and secure. The battery should not wiggle or move when you gently tug on it. If it moves, remove it and reinsert it more firmly.

Look at the battery. You should see LED lights on the outside (the battery indicator lights). The lights show how much charge the battery has. If most of the lights are on, your battery is fully charged and ready.

If you have multiple batteries, only put one in the drone at a time for now. You can swap batteries later between flights.

Step 4: Install the Control Sticks

The remote controller comes with two control sticks. These are the joystick-like handles you'll use to control the drone.

Look at the bottom of the remote controller. You'll see two small recessed slots on the left and right sides. These are where the control sticks go.

Take the left control stick and hold it vertically. Look at the bottom of the stick. You'll see a connector that looks like a small cross or plus shape.

Position the stick above the left slot. Align the connector with the slot opening and gently push the stick straight down into the slot. You should feel it click into place. The stick will be seated firmly and won't wobble.

Repeat this for the right control stick, inserting it into the right slot.

Test both sticks by moving them in all directions. They should move smoothly without any grinding sounds or resistance. They should return to the center position when you release them.

If a stick feels stiff or makes grinding sounds, remove it and check for dirt in the slot. Clean the slot gently with a soft cloth and try again.

Step 5: Unfold the Drone's Four Arms

The drone is currently in its folded, compact position. You need to unfold all four arms to prepare it for flight.

The drone has four arms: front-left, front-right, back-left, and back-right. When folded, the arms lie flat against the main body.

Start with the front arms. Hold the main body of the drone steady with one hand. With your other hand, grab the front-left arm and pull it outward and away from the body until it's perpendicular (at a 90-degree angle) to the body. You should hear a click sound when it locks into place. Repeat this for the front-right arm.

Now unfold the back arms the same way. Pull the back-left arm outward until it clicks. Then pull the back-right arm outward until it clicks.

All four arms should now be fully extended and locked. They should not fold back in if you gently push on them. This locked position is the normal flying position.

Look at the propellers at the end of each arm. They should all be pointing upward (not folded down). If any propeller is pointing to the side or down, it didn't lock correctly. Gently nudge the arm to make sure it locks fully.

Step 6: Unfold the Antennas

The remote controller has two antennas that fold out from the top corners. These antennas send and receive signals between the controller and the drone.

Look at the top of the remote controller. You'll see two small antenna stubs on the left and right sides.

Hold the controller in your hands. With your thumbs, gently pull each antenna upward and outward. The antennas should fold up and out until they're pointing straight up vertically.

The antennas should be perpendicular to the controller (standing straight up). This position gives you the best signal range.

If you're traveling or storing the drone, you can fold the antennas back down, but always unfold them before you try to fly.

Your Pre-Flight Checklist

Before you power on your drone for the first time, you need to check that everything is assembled correctly and ready to fly safely. This checklist is critical. Go through each item and make sure everything passes.

Visual Battery Check

Look at the battery installed in the drone. You should see LED indicator lights on the side. Press the small button on the battery to check its charge status. All four lights should be on (fully charged) or at least three lights should be on. If fewer than three lights are on, remove the battery and charge it fully before flying.

Propeller Check

Look at each propeller. Spin each one gently with your finger. It should spin smoothly and freely. Look carefully for any cracks, splits, or bending. If any propeller is damaged, remove it and replace it with a new one from your spare parts. Damaged propellers can cause the drone to fly unstably or dangerously.

Also check that each propeller is fully attached. Gently tug on each propeller to make sure it doesn't come off. It should be firmly locked.

Arm Check

Look at all four arms. Each arm should be fully extended and locked in the perpendicular position. Gently try to fold an arm back in. It should resist and not move. If an arm feels loose or can be easily folded back, it's not locked correctly. Unfold it and make sure you hear the click.

Gimbal and Camera Check

This is critical. Look at the front of the drone where the camera is. You should see the camera lens clearly—a small glass circle with a dark center. The camera should not be covered by any plastic.

Gently move the gimbal left and right using the left dial on the remote controller (even though the drone isn't powered on yet, the gimbal may move). The gimbal should move smoothly. Move it slowly from far left to far right and back to center.

Now look at the camera and gimbal area. There should be no cracks, no loose parts, and no damage.

Control Stick Check

Hold the remote controller with both hands. Move the left control stick upward, downward, left, and right. It should move smoothly in all directions and return to center when you release it.

Move the right control stick in all directions the same way. It should also move smoothly without any grinding sounds.

If a stick feels sticky or makes odd sounds, stop. Don't fly. Contact DJI support.

Landing Feet Check

Look at the bottom of the drone. You should see four small rubber or plastic pads under the main body. These are the landing feet.

Check each landing foot. They should be intact with no cracks or missing pieces. If a landing foot is damaged, the drone might tilt when landing.

Controller Battery Check

Look at the remote controller. On the back, you should see small LED lights showing the controller's battery level. These look like a series of small lights filling in like a battery indicator.

Press the power button once (a single press, not the hold). The lights should indicate the battery level. If only one or two lights are on, the controller battery is very low. Charge the controller before flying. For your first flight, aim for at least half-full, shown by two or more lights.

Lens Cleanliness Check

Look at the camera lens on the front of the drone. The lens should be clear and clean. You should not see dust, fingerprints, or scratches.

If the lens is dirty, gently clean it with a soft, microfiber cloth. Wipe gently in circular motions from the center outward. Do not press hard.

Gimbal Protector Final Check

Look at the front of the drone one more time. Confirm that the gimbal protector is completely removed. No plastic should be visible covering the camera. This is essential. If the protector is still there, the camera will be blocked.

Understanding What Happens Next

You've now assembled your drone and verified that everything is ready. The drone is in its flying position with arms extended, propellers attached, and battery installed.

In the next chapter, we'll cover the first power-on sequence. You'll learn how to turn on the drone correctly, how to launch the DJI Fly app on the controller, and how to go through the first-time activation process.

But before you move to the next chapter, take a moment. Look at your fully assembled drone. Hold it gently. Get comfortable with how it feels. Understand where each part is.

Run through the pre-flight checklist one more time from memory. Try to name each part without looking at this guide. The more familiar you are with the physical drone, the safer and more confident you'll feel when you fly it.

Storing Your Drone Safely

If you need to store your drone before moving to the next chapter, always reattach the gimbal protector. This is crucial for protecting the delicate camera and gimbal system.

To reattach the gimbal protector, carefully align it with the front of the drone and slide it onto the gimbal until it's fully seated. The tab should face downward.

Store your drone in a cool, dry place. Don't store it in direct sunlight or in a hot environment. A closet, cabinet, or padded bag works well.

Keep the controller and batteries in the same storage area, and make sure everything is kept dry.

Chapter 6

Battery System Deep Dive - The Intelligent Batteries

Battery Anatomy

The LiPo Cells, The Smart Chip Inside, Thermal Management

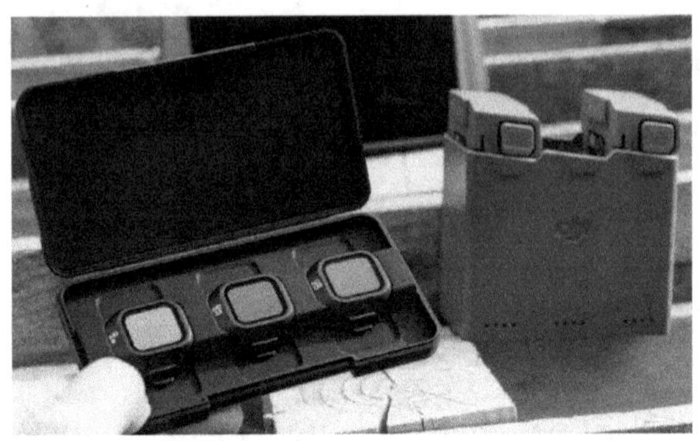

The Intelligent Flight Battery in your DJI Mini 5 Pro kit is not a simple power source. It's a sophisticated piece of technology that constantly monitors itself and communicates with your drone to ensure safe, efficient operation.

Inside the battery casing, there are LiPo (Lithium Polymer) cells. These cells store electrical energy that powers your drone. The Mini 5 Pro battery uses multiple LiPo cells connected in series to provide the required voltage and capacity. LiPo technology is chosen because it offers high energy density (a lot of power in a small package) and can discharge power quickly, which is what a drone needs.

The nominal voltage of the Mini 5 Pro battery is 7.7 volts. This voltage is standard for this drone model and is what the motors, gimbal, and electronics are designed to operate at. The battery capacity is 2250 mAh (milliamp-hours), which determines how long the battery can power the drone.

Beyond just LiPo cells, each battery contains an embedded smart chip. This chip is a small computer inside the battery. The smart chip monitors multiple parameters in real-time:

It measures the voltage across the battery cells. Voltage tells the chip how much electrical potential is available.

It measures the temperature of the battery. The chip has internal temperature sensors that constantly check how hot the battery is getting.

It monitors the discharge current. The chip knows how much power is being drawn from the battery at any moment.

It tracks the total charge capacity. Over time, LiPo batteries lose some capacity as they age. The smart chip remembers the battery's health and communicates this information to the drone and the DJI Fly app.

The smart chip also provides safety protections. If the battery gets too hot, the chip can disable discharge to prevent damage. If the voltage drops too low, the chip prevents over-discharge, which would permanently damage the battery.

The battery also has a thermal management system. This is not a cooling fan. Instead, it's a system of internal structures designed to dissipate heat. The battery casing and internal layout are designed to spread heat evenly and dissipate it as efficiently as possible. This keeps the battery at a safe temperature during normal operation.

When you fly your drone on a hot day, or when you fly multiple batteries back-to-back without giving the batteries time to cool, the thermal management system helps prevent the battery from overheating. However, if the battery gets too hot, the smart chip may throttle (reduce) power output or refuse to discharge to protect itself.

How to Identify Battery Health: LEDs on the Battery, Percentage Indicators

Each battery has four LED indicator lights on one end. These lights are the battery's way of telling you its current charge level without needing to plug it into anything or use the app.

The LEDs are small, circular lights arranged in a row. They're located on the end of the battery that has the contacts (the metal connectors). This is the end that plugs into the drone.

To check the battery's charge level at any time, press the small button on the side of the battery. When you press this button, the LED lights will briefly illuminate to show you the current charge status.

If all four LED lights are on, the battery is fully charged at 100 percent. This is the ideal state before flying.

If three LED lights are on, the battery is at approximately 75 percent charge. This is still good and safe to fly with.

If two LED lights are on, the battery is at approximately 50 percent charge. The battery is usable but not optimal for long flights.

If only one LED light is on, the battery is at approximately 25 percent charge. This is considered low battery. You should charge it soon. While you can still fly with this charge, your flight time will be short.

If no LED lights are on when you press the button, the battery is either completely dead (0 percent) or there's a problem with the battery. A dead battery should be charged immediately. If the battery won't show any lights even after pressing the button for a few seconds, there may be an issue.

The LED indicator is very useful because you can check the battery charge level without needing power, without needing the controller, and without using the app. You can quickly look at a battery sitting in your gear bag and know if it's ready to fly.

In the DJI Fly app, you can also see the battery percentage as a more precise number (like 82 percent, 63 percent, etc.) when the battery is installed in the drone and powered on. The app shows the battery health and sometimes shows a "battery health" percentage that indicates how much capacity the battery retains compared to when it was new. A battery at 80 percent health is still fine; below 70 percent health, consider replacing the battery.

Charging at Home

Using the Charging Hub, How Long It Takes (1.5 Hours), Temperature Requirements

The charging hub is the primary way to charge your batteries at home. The hub can charge up to three batteries simultaneously, which is very convenient if you have multiple batteries.

The charging hub is a rectangular device with three battery slots. Each slot is designed to hold one battery. The hub also has a USB-C charging port on the bottom where you connect the power cable.

To charge a battery using the hub, insert the battery into one of the three slots. The battery slides in with the contact end (metal connectors) facing down into the slot. The battery will click into place when fully inserted. Don't force it. If it doesn't slide in smoothly, the battery orientation might be wrong. Flip it and try again.

Once the battery is in the slot, you can see the LED indicator lights on the side of the battery. These lights will show you the charge status of that specific battery.

To power the hub and begin charging, plug the USB-C cable into the charging port on the bottom of the hub. The other end of the cable connects to a USB power adapter (usually a 5V or 9V adapter) that plugs into wall power.

When charging begins, the hub will have indicator lights showing the charge status of each battery. These lights are usually on the hub itself, separate from the battery's LED lights. The hub's lights typically show:

Green light or steady light means the battery is charging normally.

Amber or yellow light might indicate a slower charge or a warning condition.

Red light might indicate an error or problem with that battery.

The charging process for a single battery takes approximately 1.5 to 2 hours using the standard charging hub with a 5V/2A power adapter. If you're charging three batteries simultaneously, each individual battery still takes about 1.5 to 2 hours, so all three batteries will be fully charged after that time.

If you use a higher wattage power adapter (like a 9V/3A adapter), the charging might be slightly faster, but the overall time is still around 1.5 hours per battery.

Temperature requirements are important for safe charging. The ideal temperature range for charging is between 50 degrees Fahrenheit (10 degrees Celsius) and 104 degrees Fahrenheit (40 degrees Celsius).

If the ambient temperature is too cold (below 50 degrees Fahrenheit), the charging process will be much slower or may not work at all. The chemical reactions inside the LiPo cells slowdown in cold temperatures, preventing efficient charging. Never try to charge a battery that feels very cold to the touch. Let it warm up naturally to room temperature first.

If the ambient temperature is too hot (above 104 degrees Fahrenheit), the battery might refuse to charge or charge very slowly. The smart chip inside the battery will sense the high temperature and limit charging to protect the battery from overheating and potential damage.

Always charge in a room-temperature environment. Your home, garage, or indoor workspace is ideal. Do not charge batteries in direct sunlight, in a hot car, or in freezing outdoor conditions.

Charging on the Go:

USB-C Portable Power Bank Method, What Wattage to Use

If you're flying away from home and need to charge batteries without access to a charging hub, you can use a portable USB-C power bank.

A portable power bank is a battery pack that stores electrical energy and can charge devices via USB. Many modern power banks have USB-C ports, making them compatible with the DJI charging system.

To charge a battery with a power bank, you need a USB-C cable. Connect one end of the USB-C cable to the power bank's USB-C output port. Connect the other end to the battery's charging port (the same port where you'd plug in the charging hub cable).

The battery will begin charging immediately. The LED lights on the battery will show the charge status as before. You can also disconnect and reconnect the power bank to check the charge level without losing the charging session.

The wattage of the power bank is important. The term "wattage" refers to the power output of the power bank.

A power bank with 5V/2A output is adequate for slow charging of a single battery.

A power bank with 9V/2A or higher output will charge the battery faster, closer to the normal 1.5-hour charging speed.

Avoid using power banks with extremely high wattage outputs (like 20V or higher) because these are designed for larger devices and might damage the battery's smart chip or cause overcharging.

The ideal power bank for charging DJI batteries is one with USB-C output rated at 5V-9V and 2-3 amperes.

Practical tip: If you're flying away from home and expect to need multiple flights, bring either the charging hub (if you have access to wall power) or a large capacity power bank (at least 15,000 mAh capacity) so you can charge multiple batteries between flights.

Battery Storage

Long-Term Storage Rules (Charge Every 3 Months), Temperature Range

If you're not planning to fly for an extended period, proper battery storage is essential to maintain battery health.

LiPo batteries should not be stored in a fully charged state. Storing a fully charged battery at room temperature causes the battery to slowly self-discharge and can degrade the cells over time. Similarly, storing a fully discharged battery (0 percent charge) can cause the battery to over-discharge internally, damaging the cells permanently.

The ideal storage charge level is approximately 50 percent. Before storing a battery for more than a few weeks, charge it to about 50 percent (which would show 2 out of 4 LED lights). Then disconnect it and store it.

The ideal storage temperature range is between 41 degrees Fahrenheit (5 degrees Celsius) and 77 degrees Fahrenheit (25 degrees Celsius). Room temperature is perfect. A closet, cabinet, or drawer in your home is an ideal storage location.

Do not store batteries in extreme heat (like an attic in summer) or extreme cold (like an unheated garage in winter). Extreme temperatures degrade battery cells.

Do not store batteries in humid environments. Moisture can corrode the battery contacts and damage the smart chip.

Long-term storage rules state that you should charge each battery fully at least once every three months, even if you haven't been flying. This "maintenance charge" helps keep the battery healthy.

So if you're storing batteries over winter (three months without flying), before the three-month mark, charge each battery fully, then let it self-discharge back to 50 percent for storage. When flying resumes after three months, charge the battery fully again before use.

If you store a battery for longer than a year without any charging or flying, the battery may lose so much capacity that it becomes unsafe. After a year of storage, consider replacing old batteries with new ones.

What "Self-Heating" Means: Why the Battery Warns You in Cold Weather, How to Use It Safely

In very cold weather, the DJI Fly app might show a warning message about the battery temperature being too low. The app might also offer a "self-heating" option.

Self-heating is a feature where the battery's smart chip causes the battery to warm itself by running a small electrical current through itself. This generates heat internally.

The battery does this to warm up the LiPo cells to a temperature where they can function safely and deliver power efficiently. Cold LiPo cells cannot discharge power effectively, so warming them is necessary for flight.

If you see the self-heating prompt or warning, the app will ask if you want to enable self-heating. You can tap "Yes" to allow the battery to warm itself. The battery will warm up over a few minutes. During this time, the battery will appear in the app as "charging" even though you haven't connected a charger. This is the self-heating process.

Once the battery is warm enough, the app will indicate that it's ready to fly. At this point, you can safely use the battery for flight.

To use self-heating safely, you must have the battery installed in the drone. Do not attempt to self-heat a battery that's sitting on a table or in your hands. The self-heating process should only happen while the battery is in the drone, where thermal management systems can help dissipate the generated heat safely.

Also, self-heating consumes some battery charge, so you won't get a full flight after self-heating. Plan for a slightly shorter flight time if you used self-heating before takeoff.

If the weather is extremely cold (below 32 degrees Fahrenheit), self-heating might not be sufficient to warm the battery enough for safe flight. In extreme cold, the battery might refuse to discharge at all, and you won't be able to fly until the battery warms up naturally indoors.

Battery Safety Warnings: When NOT to Use the Battery, Swelling/Damage Signs

There are specific conditions where you should not use a battery, even if it appears to have charge.

Never use a battery that has been exposed to water or moisture. If a battery gets wet, do not attempt to charge it or use it. The moisture can cause internal short circuits. Set it aside in a safe area and let it dry completely for at least 24 hours. If moisture got inside the battery casing, it's permanently damaged and should be disposed of responsibly.

Never use a battery that has been dropped, crushed, or physically damaged. Even if the battery appears to work and the LEDs light up, internal damage might not be obvious. Internal damage can cause the battery to suddenly fail or catch fire during flight or charging. If a battery has been dropped from height or run over by a vehicle, discard it.

Never use a battery that has become swollen or puffy. Swelling is a sign of internal chemical reaction failure. A swollen battery is extremely dangerous and could catch fire or explode. If you notice a battery that looks puffy or is noticeably thicker than it should be, do not use it. Do not attempt to charge it. Place it in a safe, open area (outside is best) and allow it to discharge on its own. Never force a swollen battery to discharge faster.

Never use a battery that won't hold a charge. If a battery drains to 0 percent within a very short time of being charged, or if it shows full charge one moment and zero charge the next, there's an internal failure. Discard the battery.

Never use a battery that produces unusual sounds, smells, or leaks liquid. Any of these signs indicate a serious internal failure. Stop using the battery immediately and place it in a safe location outside.

Never leave a charging battery unattended. While charging is normally safe, batteries can malfunction. If a battery overheats during charging and fails, it's better to be nearby to respond. Never charge a battery overnight or when you're sleeping. Charge your batteries when you're awake and can monitor them.

Never force a battery into a slot or connection point. Batteries are designed to fit smoothly. If a battery doesn't slide in easily, it's oriented wrong or there's a problem. Remove it and try again with the correct orientation.

Never attempt to repair or open a battery. The internal components are not user-serviceable. If a battery needs repair, it must be handled by an authorized service center.

Flight Time Calculator: How Long You Can Fly (Roughly 19-23 Minutes Based on Conditions)

The flight time you get from a fully charged battery depends on multiple conditions. The nominal flight time for the Mini 5 Pro is approximately 19 to 23 minutes.

However, this flight time varies based on several factors:

Wind speed is the primary factor. On a calm day with no wind, you might achieve close to 23 minutes of flight time. With a headwind (wind blowing against the drone), the motors have to work harder, and flight time drops. With a strong wind (over 10 mph), flight time could drop to 19 minutes or even less.

Flying style matters. Smooth, gentle flying uses less power. Aggressive flying with rapid climbs, fast speeds, and sharp turns uses more power and reduces flight time. Beginners should expect shorter flight times because they often fly more aggressively while learning.

Temperature affects flight time. On a cold day (below 50 degrees Fahrenheit), the battery's internal resistance increases, reducing efficiency and lowering flight time. On a hot day (above 77 degrees Fahrenheit), the battery might thermally throttle its output, also reducing flight time.

Altitude affects the drone's efficiency. Flying at higher altitudes means thinner air and less efficient flight. Staying below 400 feet (120 meters) helps maximize flight time.

Payload affects flight time. If you're flying with additions or modifications (though this is not recommended for beginners), extra weight reduces flight time.

Gimbal movements and camera operation use power, though the amount is small. Using zoom, recording video, and frequent gimbal adjustments use slightly more power than static camera positioning.

Battery age affects flight time. A brand-new battery might give you the full 23 minutes. After a year of regular use, the same battery might only give you 20-21 minutes due to natural capacity loss.

Practical flight time calculator:

For a calm day, ideal conditions: Plan on about 20-22 minutes of actual flight time.

For windy conditions: Plan on about 18-20 minutes.

For very cold weather (below 40 degrees): Plan on about 17-19 minutes.

For aggressive flying style: Plan on about 18-20 minutes.

For smooth, gentle flying: Plan on about 20-23 minutes.

Important safety rule: Do not fly until the battery is completely empty. Always land when the battery reaches 20-30 percent charge remaining. This ensures you have power to safely descend and land. Flying until 0 percent risks the drone dropping out of the sky due to power loss.

Chapter 7

Propellers, Motors & Flight System

Propeller Types

The Specific Mini 5 Pro Props, Why You Can't Use Other DJI Props

The DJI Mini 5 Pro uses specific propellers that are designed for this drone model. You cannot simply use propellers from other DJI drones, even if they look similar. Using incorrect propellers can cause the drone to fly erratically or not at all.

The Mini 5 Pro propellers come in two types, determined by their rotation direction:

Clockwise rotating propellers (usually marked with a single line or specific color on one blade) spin in the clockwise direction when viewed from above. These are installed on the front-left and rear-right motors.

Counterclockwise rotating propellers (usually marked with two lines or a different color on one blade) spin in the counterclockwise direction when viewed from above. These are installed on the front-right and rear-left motors.

This alternating pattern is intentional. When two propellers on opposite corners spin in opposite directions, they create a balanced lift system that prevents the drone from spinning uncontrollably.

Why you can't use other DJI props: Propellers are engineered specifically for each drone model. The blade shape, length, pitch (angle of the blades), and weight are all calculated for the Mini 5 Pro's specific motors and flight characteristics. Using propellers from a different DJI model (like a Mini 3 or Air 3) would:

Create thrust imbalance, making the drone fly unstably or tilt to one side.

Cause the motors to work harder than designed, draining battery faster.

Potentially cause vibration that makes video shaky and photos blurry.
Damage the motors over time due to excessive load.
In extreme cases, prevent the drone from flying at all.
The Mini 5 Pro propeller model number should be marked on the blades or in the drone documentation. If you need to replace propellers, order the exact Mini 5 Pro replacement propellers from DJI or an authorized dealer.

Propeller Installation:

Step-by-Step (Clockwise vs Counterclockwise, The Click Sound)
Installing propellers correctly is essential for safe flight. Incorrectly installed propellers can come loose during flight, causing a crash.
Before you start, identify which propellers go where. Look at the markings on the propeller blades. Clockwise propellers have one marking (usually a single line or dot), and counterclockwise propellers have two markings.
Step 1: Position the drone so you can clearly see all four motors. Each motor is at the end of an arm. The motors are metal cylinders with a shaft sticking up.
Step 2: Look at the motor shaft on the front-left position. Take a clockwise propeller (single marking). Hold it vertically so the shaft goes through the center hole of the propeller.
Step 3: Position the propeller directly above the motor shaft. The propeller will only fit one way due to a notch or key in the center hole. Align the propeller with the shaft.
Step 4: Gently push the propeller straight down onto the shaft. You're not forcing it hard—just steady, straight down pressure. As you push, you'll feel the propeller slide onto the shaft.
Step 5: Keep pushing until you hear and feel a click. This click is critical. It means the propeller has fully seated and is locked in place. The click is the

locking mechanism engaging. Do not stop pushing before you feel the click.

Step 6: Gently tug on the propeller to confirm it's locked. It should not come off. It should not move around on the shaft. If it wiggles or comes loose, remove it and try again—you didn't push far enough to trigger the click.

Step 7: Repeat this process for the front-right motor with a counterclockwise propeller (two markings).

Step 8: Move to the rear-left motor and install a counterclockwise propeller the same way.

Step 9: Install a clockwise propeller on the rear-right motor.

After all four propellers are installed, manually spin each propeller by hand. They should spin smoothly and freely. If any propeller feels stiff or grinds, there's a problem. Stop and check the installation.

The click sound is absolutely critical. It's your confirmation that the propeller is fully locked. Never fly without being certain all propellers are fully clicked in place.

Storage & Replacement

How Many Spares to Carry, When to Replace Them (Cracks, Bends, Wear)

Propellers break. It's part of drone flying. Even gentle crashes or collisions can damage propellers. Always carry spares.

Recommended spare quantity: Carry at least 2 to 4 extra propellers when you go flying. A single propeller is enough for a single emergency replacement, but two pairs (four total) is better because you might need to replace propellers multiple times in a day.

Your kit likely came with spare propellers. Keep them in a protective bag in your flying kit.

When to replace a propeller: Inspect propellers before every flight. Look for:

Cracks or splits in the blade: Even a small crack will worsen as the propeller spins. A cracked propeller can break mid-flight, causing the drone to drop. Replace immediately.

Bends in the blade: A bent propeller is out of balance, creating vibration and potentially causing a crash. Replace bent propellers.

Chunks missing from the blade: Damage from a crash or impact. Replace if any part of the blade is broken away.

Discoloration or burn marks: Usually indicates the propeller hit something and got hot. The material might be weakened. Replace if significant.

General wear: After months of flying, propellers gradually degrade. The blade edges might become rough or the balance might drift slightly. If you notice your videos becoming shakier or the drone becoming harder to control, worn propellers might be the cause. Replace them.

Always err on the side of caution with propellers. They're inexpensive compared to a damaged drone. If a propeller looks questionable, replace it.

Storage of spare propellers: Keep them in a bag or container that protects them from bending or breaking. Propeller blade covers or foam inserts help prevent damage during transport.

Motor System: Four Brushless Motors,

What They Do, Listening for Unusual Sounds

The DJI Mini 5 Pro has four brushless motors, one at the end of each arm. These motors are the engines that power the propellers.

Brushless motors are called "brushless" because they don't have brushes (electrical contacts that wear out). Brushless motors are more efficient, quieter, and more reliable than older "brushed" motor designs. They're the standard for modern drones.

What the motors do: Each motor spins its propeller at high speed (thousands of revolutions per minute). The spinning propellers push air downward, creating lift that raises the drone into the air. By controlling the speed of each motor independently, the flight control system can tilt the drone forward, backward, left, right, or rotate it.

Motor sounds: When the drone is operating normally, you'll hear the distinctive whirring sound of the propellers spinning. This is normal and expected. The motor sound should be smooth and consistent.

Unusual sounds to listen for:

Grinding noise: This sounds like grinding or scraping, indicating something is wrong with the motor. Stop flying immediately.

Clicking or popping: Irregular clicking sounds suggest a mechanical problem inside the motor. Land the drone and don't fly until the issue is identified.

Buzzing: A buzzing sound different from the normal whir might indicate a damaged propeller or bent blade. Inspect propellers.

Loud whining: A high-pitched whine that's louder than normal might indicate the motor is under excessive strain. Land immediately.

Inconsistent speeds: If you hear one propeller spinning noticeably faster or slower than the others, there's a motor issue. Land the drone.

If you notice any unusual sounds, land the drone immediately. Continue flying with damaged motors risks the drone dropping out of the sky due to motor failure.

Motor testing: Before every flight, the drone's self-diagnostic system tests all motors during startup. If a motor fails the test, the app will show an error message. Do not fly if there are motor errors.

Arm Folding Mechanism

How to Fold/Unfold All Four Arms, The Automatic Power-On Feature
The DJI Mini 5 Pro's arms fold in and out, making the drone compact for transport but extending for flight stability.

How the mechanism works: Each arm is connected to the main body with a hinge. The arms fold inward (flat against the body) for storage and unfold outward (perpendicular to the body) for flight.

How to unfold the arms for flight:

Step 1: Hold the drone with the body horizontal, arms folded against the sides.

Step 2: Grab the front-left arm near where it meets the body. Pull it outward and away from the body until it's perpendicular (at a 90-degree angle) to the body. You should feel and hear a click as the arm locks into place.

Step 3: Repeat for the front-right arm.

Step 4: Move to the rear arms. Pull the rear-left arm outward until you hear the click.

Step 5: Unfold the rear-right arm the same way.

All four arms should now be fully extended and locked. They should not fold back if you gently push them. The locked position is the normal flying position.

Important: The automatic power-on feature is triggered when you unfold the rear-right arm (or the rear-left arm on some configurations). When you unfold this arm fully and lock it, the drone will automatically power on without you needing to press the power button. This is convenient but means you need to be ready when you unfold that arm—the drone will spring to life.

How to fold the arms for storage:

Step 1: Hold the drone with arms extended in the flight position.

Step 2: Grab the front-left arm and pull it back toward the body until it folds flat against the side. You might hear a click as it releases and folds.

Step 3: Repeat for each of the other three arms.

All arms should now be folded flat against the body, making the drone compact and safe for transport.

Important during folding: Be gentle. The hinge mechanism is designed to lock but shouldn't be forced. If an arm resists folding or unfolding, check that there are no obstructions and don't use excessive force.

The arm locking mechanism is crucial for flight stability. Never fly with an arm that isn't fully extended and locked. Never fly with an arm in a partially folded or intermediate position.

Landing Gear

Understanding the Fixed Landing Feet, Height Off Ground

The DJI Mini 5 Pro has four fixed landing feet. These are small pads or stands underneath the main body. They don't fold in or out—they're always extended.

Purpose of landing feet: The landing feet protect the main body of the drone from touching the ground. Without them, the camera, battery compartment, and electronics would be in direct contact with the ground, risking damage.

Height off ground: The landing feet raise the drone approximately 1 to 2 inches (2.5 to 5 centimeters) above the ground. This clearance is enough to protect the main body and camera gimbal from ground contact.

Landing surface considerations: The landing feet are designed for relatively smooth, level surfaces. Landing on:

Soft grass: The feet sink slightly into the grass, which is fine. The drone sits securely.

Concrete or asphalt: The feet provide good grip. The hard surface is safe for landing.

Sand or gravel: The feet can sink into loose material. This is acceptable for landing, but inspect the drone after landing to ensure no sand got into air intakes.

Very rough terrain: Rocky, uneven, or sharp surfaces can damage the landing feet or tip the drone over if it lands unevenly. Avoid landing on very rough terrain.

Water: Never land on water. The landing feet are not designed to float, and the drone will sink.

Never remove or damage the landing feet. They're essential for protecting the drone. If a landing foot is broken or missing, repair or replace it before flying.

Weight & Balance

Why the Drone Weighs 248g, What This Means Legally in Many Countries

The DJI Mini 5 Pro weighs approximately 248 grams. This specific weight is important for legal reasons.

Why the weight: The battery is the heaviest single component, weighing about 73 grams. The motor and propeller assemblies add significant weight. The main body, gimbal, and camera system, combined with the electronics, bring the total to around 248 grams.

Legal significance: In many countries, drones under 250 grams have different legal requirements than heavier drones. For example:

In many regions, drones under 250 grams don't require registration with aviation authorities.

They may have fewer flight restrictions than heavier drones.

They might not require a pilot's license or certification.

Insurance requirements may be different.

The Mini 5 Pro was engineered to stay just under the 250-gram threshold in many countries, making it legally easier to operate for recreational pilots.

Important: Check your local regulations. Laws vary by country and region. Some places have different rules even for sub-250-gram drones. Do not assume that because your drone is under 250 grams, you can fly anywhere. Always research and follow local laws.

Weight and balance impact: The weight distribution affects how the drone flies. The battery weight is centered in the main body, and the motor-propeller assemblies are distributed evenly at the corners. This balance is calculated for optimal flight stability.

Never add items to the drone (like cameras or lights) not designed by DJI for the Mini 5 Pro. Adding weight changes the balance and weight distribution, affecting flight stability and potentially causing crashes.

Obstacle Avoidance Sensors

Where They Are (Forward, Backward, Downward), What They Detect

The Mini 5 Pro has multiple obstacle avoidance sensors that help the drone see and avoid obstacles automatically.

Forward-facing obstacle avoidance: On the front of the drone, below the camera, are two small cameras facing forward. These cameras continuously monitor the area directly ahead of the drone as it flies forward. If they detect an obstacle (a tree, building, person, or other object), they send signals to the flight control system to slow the drone down, stop it, or avoid the obstacle.

Backward-facing obstacle avoidance: On the back of the drone are two cameras facing backward. These activate when the drone is flying in reverse (backward). They serve the same function as the forward cameras but for backward flight.

Downward-facing obstacle avoidance: Underneath the drone, pointing straight down, are two cameras. These serve multiple purposes:

They detect the ground and help the drone maintain altitude.

They assist in landing by detecting suitable landing surfaces.

They help with the LiDAR sensor (described below) to measure precise altitude.

They detect obstacles below the drone (though not all downward obstacles can be detected).

LiDAR sensor: The Mini 5 Pro also has a LiDAR (Light Detection and Ranging) sensor, which is more advanced than camera-based obstacle avoidance. The LiDAR sensor uses lasers to measure distance to objects. It's more accurate than cameras, especially in low light or when flying over uniform surfaces (like snow or sand where cameras struggle to detect obstacles). The LiDAR sensor is located on the bottom of the drone and provides precise altitude measurement and ground-based obstacle detection.

How obstacle avoidance works: These sensors constantly scan the environment in real-time. The data feeds into the flight control system's decision-making algorithms. If an obstacle is detected:

In Brake mode: The drone stops moving and hovers in place, waiting for your input.

In Bypass mode: The drone slows down but doesn't stop, allowing you to maintain control while being warned of obstacles.

You can configure which mode to use in the DJI Fly app settings.

Limitations of obstacle avoidance: Obstacle avoidance is a safety feature, but it's not perfect. Limitations include:

It doesn't detect very small obstacles (thin branches, wires).

In very dark conditions, camera-based detection is reduced (LiDAR works better).

Very transparent materials (glass windows, clear plastic) can be hard to detect.

Extreme weather (heavy rain, snow) can reduce sensor effectiveness.

Fast speeds make obstacle detection more difficult (hence obstacle avoidance is disabled in Sport mode).

Never rely solely on obstacle avoidance to keep the drone safe. Always maintain visual line of sight, fly in appropriate conditions, and take personal responsibility for avoiding obstacles.

Pre-Flight Motor Test

Before every flight, the drone tests the motors during the startup sequence. During this test, you'll hear brief spinning sounds from each motor as the system verifies they're working correctly. This is normal and expected. If the test fails, the app will show an error, and you should not fly.

Chapter 8

Control Stick Modes - Finding Your Flying Style

Mode 1 (Japanese): Left Stick = Altitude/Rotation, Right Stick = Forward/Back/Left/Right

Mode 1, also known as Japanese mode, is less commonly used today but is still available as an option. It's historically preferred by some helicopter pilots.

In Mode 1:

The left control stick controls two dimensions simultaneously:

Moving the stick up makes the drone ascend (go higher).

Moving the stick down makes the drone descend (go lower).

Moving the stick left makes the drone rotate counterclockwise (spin left).

Moving the stick right makes the drone rotate clockwise (spin right).

This combination is called "throttle and yaw" control. Throttle is the up-down altitude control, and yaw is the rotation around the vertical axis.

The right control stick controls forward, backward, left, and right movement:

Moving the stick forward makes the drone pitch forward and fly forward away from you.

Moving the stick backward makes the drone pitch backward and fly backward toward you.

Moving the stick left makes the drone roll left and fly left.

Moving the stick right makes the drone roll right and fly right.

This combination is called "roll and pitch" control. Roll is the left-right tilt, and pitch is the forward-backward tilt.

Why Mode 1 is less common now:

Most modern drone pilots and YouTube tutorials use Mode 2.

Helicopter pilots sometimes preferred Mode 1 because traditional helicopter controls worked similarly.

For new drone pilots, Mode 1 is harder to learn than Mode 2.

Few beginner resources exist for Mode 1.

Mode 2 (American/Standard - DEFAULT): Left Stick = Altitude/Rotation, Right Stick = Forward/Back/Left/Right

Mode 2 is the default configuration on your DJI Mini 5 Pro controller. It's the most commonly used mode worldwide and is the standard for most modern drone pilots.

In Mode 2 (your current configuration):

The left control stick controls:

Moving up: Drone ascends.

Moving down: Drone descends.

Moving left: Drone rotates counterclockwise (spins left).

Moving right: Drone rotates clockwise (spins right).

Like Mode 1, this is throttle and yaw control.

The right control stick controls:

Moving forward: Drone pitches forward and flies forward.

Moving backward: Drone pitches backward and flies backward.

Moving left: Drone rolls left and flies left.

Moving right: Drone rolls right and flies right.

This is roll and pitch control, just like Mode 1.

The key difference: Mode 2 comes pre-configured, and this is what you'll use unless you specifically change it.

Advantages of Mode 2:

It's the industry standard. Almost all YouTube tutorials use Mode 2.

Most drone pilots use Mode 2, so if you learn Mode 2, you can easily use other people's drones or help from experienced pilots.

It's intuitive: the stick that controls altitude (left) is separate from the stick that controls movement direction (right).

Most resources and guides assume Mode 2.

Why Mode 2 feels natural:

For pilots who have experience with video game controllers, Mode 2 feels similar to how console games map controls—left stick for one set of actions, right stick for another.

The separation of functions (altitude on left, direction on right) makes it easier to learn the basic concepts before combining movements.

Mode 3 (Chinese): Right Stick = Altitude/Rotation, Left Stick = Forward/Back/Left/Right

Mode 3, also known as Chinese mode, is the opposite of Mode 1. It's less common in Western countries but preferred by some pilots, particularly in China.

In Mode 3:

The left control stick controls forward, backward, left, and right movement:

Moving forward: Drone flies forward.

Moving backward: Drone flies backward.

Moving left: Drone flies left.

Moving right: Drone flies right.

The right control stick controls altitude and rotation:

Moving up: Drone ascends.

Moving down: Drone descends.

Moving left: Drone rotates counterclockwise.

Moving right: Drone rotates clockwise.

This is essentially Mode 1 with the sticks reversed.

Why Mode 3 exists:

Some pilots find it more intuitive to control altitude with their right hand (dominant hand for most people).

It's popular in certain regions, particularly China, where it became the local standard.

Disadvantages for beginners:

Very few English-language tutorials use Mode 3.

Most online resources assume Mode 2.

If you switch to Mode 3, you'll have a harder time following along with most educational videos.

How to Change Modes

Go to Camera View > Settings > Control > Control Mode

Changing your control mode is straightforward and can be done at any time, even on the same day.

Step-by-step process:

Step 1: Launch the DJI Fly app and ensure you're connected to your drone and controller.

Step 2: On the main flight screen, look for the Settings icon. This is usually a gear symbol (⚙) located in the top-right corner of the screen.

Step 3: Tap the Settings icon. A menu will open showing various settings categories.

Step 4: Scroll down through the menu until you find an option labeled "Control," "Control Settings," or "Remote Controller Settings."

Step 5: Tap on "Control" to open the control settings menu.

Step 6: In the Control Settings menu, look for an option called "Control Mode," "Flight Mode," or "Stick Mode."

Step 7: Tap on this option. You'll see three choices:

Mode 1 (Japanese)

Mode 2 (American/Standard)

Mode 3 (Chinese)

Step 8: Select your preferred mode by tapping on it.

Step 9: The app will confirm your selection. Some versions may ask you to confirm the change.

Step 10: The new mode takes effect immediately. You do not need to restart the app, controller, or drone.

Optional: After changing modes, it's a good idea to test the new configuration by doing a brief hover test before flying to make sure you're comfortable with the new stick layout.

Navigation tip: If you have trouble finding these settings, remember that the settings path is usually:

Main Flight Screen → Settings (⚙ icon) → Control → Control Mode

Why Mode Matters

Personal Preference, What Most YouTube Tutorials Use (Mode 2)

Your choice of control mode is fundamentally a personal preference, but there are practical considerations.

Personal preference:

Some people naturally prefer one mode over another based on their previous experience.

If you've played video games with a controller, Mode 2 might feel more natural.

If you've flown helicopters or RC aircraft before, you might have a preference based on that experience.

The best mode is the one that feels most intuitive to your hands and brain.

YouTube tutorials and online resources:

The overwhelming majority of drone tutorials on YouTube use Mode 2. This is a significant practical advantage.

When you watch a tutorial and the instructor says "push the right stick forward," if you're using Mode 2, you'll know exactly what that means.

If you're using Mode 1 or Mode 3, you'll constantly be translating the instructions mentally, which is confusing and error-prone.

Professional pilots and instructors:

Mode 2 is the industry standard for commercial drone pilots and instructors.

If you ever take formal drone training or certification, it will almost certainly be in Mode 2.

If you want to join drone communities or clubs, Mode 2 is the standard they'll use.

Switching between drones:

If you ever fly another drone (a friend's drone, a rental, a different DJI model), it will almost certainly be set to Mode 2.

Knowing Mode 2 makes you adaptable across different equipment.

Switching Without Resetting

Can You Switch During the Day? (Yes, in Settings)

You can absolutely switch control modes at any time without any negative consequences. You don't need to restart the app, controller, or drone.

Practical scenarios:

Let's say you start your flying session in Mode 2 (your default).

You fly for a while and decide Mode 1 feels better to you.

You can land the drone, go into Settings > Control > Control Mode, and switch to Mode 1.

As soon as you tap Mode 1, the change takes effect.

You can take off again immediately and fly in Mode 1.

Later, if you want to switch back to Mode 2, the process is identical.

No harm in experimenting:

You can try each mode for a short flight.

If it doesn't feel right, switch back.

There are no penalties or complications for changing modes.

Some pilots even switch modes mid-day depending on the task.

Important caveat:

Once you settle on a mode, it's best to stick with it for at least several flights while you're learning.

Constantly switching modes during training confuses your muscle memory.

Let your brain build habits with one mode before switching.

After you're proficient, experimenting is fine, but consistency during the learning phase is important.

Practice Recommendation

Which Mode for Beginners, How to Get Comfortable with It

For absolute beginners, Mode 2 is the recommended starting point. Here's why and how to get comfortable with it.

Why Mode 2 for beginners:

It's your drone's default configuration—you don't need to change anything.

All beginner-friendly resources assume Mode 2.

If you get stuck and ask for help online, the advice will be for Mode 2.

Most YouTube tutorials use Mode 2.

If you ever take a drone class, it will be Mode 2.

How to get comfortable with Mode 2:

Your first few flights should be in a wide-open area with nothing to crash into (a large park, field, or empty parking lot).

Practice these movements in order:

Session 1: Just practice the left stick. Hover at a safe altitude, then practice moving the left stick up and down slowly to change altitude. Get comfortable with how fast the drone ascends and descends. Land and practice again.

Session 2: While hovering, practice the left stick left and right movements. This rotates the drone. Rotate slowly in one direction for a full circle, then rotate the other way. Get a feel for how fast the rotation is.

Session 3: Practice the right stick forward and backward movements. While hovering, gently push the right stick forward and let the drone fly forward slowly. Practice bringing it back with the right stick backward. Do this at very low altitude (5 feet or so) so if something goes wrong, you're close to the ground.

Session 4: Practice the right stick left and right movements. While hovering low, move the right stick left to fly left, then right to fly right. Keep these movements slow and gentle.

Session 5: Combine movements. Try moving both sticks together: left stick up to gain altitude while right stick forward to move forward. Practice moving diagonally.

Session 6: Practice landing. Bring the drone down with the left stick, and when near the ground, use the right stick to position it above your landing spot, then descend fully with the left stick.

Muscle memory building:

After about 5-10 flights practicing Mode 2 basics, your hands will start to understand the controls without you thinking about it consciously.

By your 10th-15th flight, your muscle memory should be strong enough that you're not consciously thinking about which stick does what.

This is the goal: automatic, instinctive control.

If you constantly switch modes, this muscle memory development is delayed.

Beginner practice guidelines:

Only practice in calm weather (low wind).

Practice in wide-open spaces with no obstacles.

Practice during daylight hours when you can clearly see the drone.

Start with very slow, gentle stick movements. Speed comes later.

Land after 10-15 minutes of flying. The batteries need rest, and your hands need breaks.

Never practice flying close to people, animals, or property.

What to expect:

Your first flight will feel clumsy. This is normal. Everyone feels this way.

You might oversteer or be jerky with the sticks. This is expected.

By your 5th flight, you'll notice significant improvement in smoothness.

By your 10th flight, you should feel reasonably comfortable and confident.

Patience is essential. Drone flying is a skill that develops with practice.

Common Beginner Mistakes with Control Modes

Over-correcting: When you make a small mistake with the sticks, the natural instinct is to over-correct. This makes the drone move too much the opposite direction. Practice smooth, gentle stick movements instead. Small inputs produce better results.

Mixing up the sticks: Early on, you might accidentally use the wrong stick for what you want. This is normal. Being conscious of "left stick for up/down and rotation" and "right stick for forward/back/left/right" helps retrain your hands.

Moving sticks too fast: Your instinct might be to move the sticks quickly to get fast results, but drone control is about finesse. Slow, gentle stick movements lead to smoother, more controlled flight.

Forgetting to alternate sticks: In actual flying, you'll often need to use both sticks simultaneously. For example, ascending while moving forward (left stick up + right stick forward). Practice these combinations.

Getting frustrated: Learning drone control takes time. Don't expect to be proficient after one or two flights. Embrace the learning process, enjoy each small improvement, and be patient with yourself.

Summary

You now understand the three control modes available on your DJI Mini 5 Pro:

Mode 1 (Japanese): Less common, throttle/yaw on left, roll/pitch on right.

Mode 2 (American/Standard): Your default mode, industry standard, recommended for beginners.

Mode 3 (Chinese): Opposite of Mode 1, less common in the West.

You know how to change modes in the DJI Fly app settings.

You understand why Mode 2 is recommended and why it matters for learning from tutorials and flying with others.

You know that you can switch modes at any time without complications.

You have a practice plan for getting comfortable with Mode 2 through structured, progressive flying sessions.

Chapter 9

The C1 & C2 Custom Buttons - Making Your Own Controls

What These Buttons Do by Default: Gimbal Functions (Recenter, Point Down)

The C1 and C2 buttons are located on the underside of the remote controller (the bottom when holding it). These buttons are customizable, but they come with sensible defaults from the factory.

Location of the buttons:

When you flip your controller upside down (hold it with the screen facing away from you), you'll see the bottom.

On the left side (your left hand) is the C1 button. It's a circular button positioned where your left hand naturally rests during flight.

On the right side (your right hand) is the C2 button, positioned symmetrically to C1.

Between them (center) is the Return to Home (RTH) button, which you learned about earlier.

Default function of C1 (Gimbal Recenter):

When you press C1, the gimbal (camera mount) instantly returns to a horizontal position (0 degrees tilt).

This is useful when you've tilted the camera up or down and want to quickly return it to looking straight ahead.

For example: You've been looking down at the ground, and you want to see the horizon again. Press C1 and the camera instantly snaps back to horizontal.

The camera doesn't gradually tilt back—it returns quickly and smoothly in about half a second.

Default function of C2 (Gimbal Point Down):

When you press C2, the gimbal tilts instantly to point straight down (minus 90 degrees, which means the camera aims directly at the ground below the drone).

This is useful for overhead shots, mapping, inspecting things on the ground, or getting a top-down view of a subject.

For example: You want to film a building from directly above. Press C2 and the camera points straight down, giving you a perfect overhead perspective.

Like C1, this movement is smooth and quick, completing in about half a second.

Why these defaults exist:

These two functions (recenter and point down) are the most commonly used gimbal movements during flight.

They provide quick access to two key gimbal positions without needing to manually tilt the gimbal using the left dial.

By pressing a button instead of rotating a dial, you can achieve these positions one-handed, with your thumb.

Even if you customize these buttons later, these defaults work great for beginners who don't need custom functions.

How to Customize Them

Camera View > Settings > Control > Button Customization (Exact Path)

Customizing the C1 and C2 buttons is straightforward. The process is the same whether you want to change C1, C2, or both.

Complete step-by-step path:

Step 1: Open the DJI Fly app and ensure you're connected to your drone and controller.

Step 2: You should be on the main camera view (the flight screen showing the live feed from the drone).

Step 3: In the top-right corner of the screen, locate the Settings icon. It looks like a gear (⚙).

Step 4: Tap the Settings icon. A menu will appear with various options.

Step 5: In the Settings menu, scroll down until you find "Control" or "Remote Controller Settings."

Step 6: Tap on "Control" to open the control settings submenu.

Step 7: In the Control submenu, scroll down and look for an option called "Button Customization," "Custom Buttons," or "Button Assignment."

Step 8: Tap on "Button Customization." You'll now see options for C1 and C2.

Step 9: To customize C1:

Tap on "C1" or "C1 Button Assignment."

A list of available functions will appear.

Select the function you want C1 to perform.

The change is saved immediately.

Step 10: To customize C2, repeat the same process by tapping on "C2" and selecting your desired function.

Step 11: Exit the settings by tapping the back arrow or home button. The new configurations are now active.

Testing your customization:

After you've set up C1 and C2, it's a good idea to test them before flying.

Press C1 while the drone is on the ground (not flying). Verify it performs the function you assigned.

Press C2 and verify it works as expected.

If a button doesn't seem to work, go back to Settings > Control > Button Customization and verify the assignment is correct.

Important notes:

The changes take effect immediately. You don't need to restart the app, controller, or drone.

You can change the button assignments as many times as you want, whenever you want.

The changes persist until you manually change them again or reset to defaults.

If you ever get confused about what a button does, return to Settings > Control > Button Customization to verify the current assignment.

Available Custom Functions: Detailed Explanation of Each

Your C1 and C2 buttons can be assigned to any of the following functions. Understand each option so you can choose the best setup for your flying style.

Camera Zoom (1x ↔ 2x switching):

What it does: Pressing this button toggles the camera zoom between 1x (normal wide view) and 2x (medium tele view). Each press switches to the other zoom level.

Why you'd want it: If you frequently switch between wide shots and zoomed shots, having a one-press button is much faster than rotating the right dial. Filmmakers who shoot both wide establishing shots and detail shots often use this.

How it feels: Press button → camera instantly snaps to 2x zoom. Press again → instantly back to 1x. No intermediate steps.

Limitation: This is a toggle (1x or 2x only). You can't access 4x zoom with this button. If you need 4x, you'll still need to use the right dial.

Camera Rotation (Portrait ↔ Landscape):

What it does: Pressing this button rotates the camera 90 degrees. A second press rotates it another 90 degrees back to the original orientation. Why you'd want it: The Mini 5 Pro can record video in both landscape (wider) and portrait (taller) orientations. This button lets you switch between them with a single tap. This is especially useful for content creators who want to film for both traditional screens and social media (where vertical video is common).

How it feels: Press button → camera smoothly rotates 90 degrees in about 0.5 seconds. The whole drone stays level; only the camera rotates. Press again → rotates back.

Use cases: Shooting a tall building? Press to portrait mode. Shooting a sunset landscape? Press to landscape mode.

Note: This feature requires your controller firmware to support it. Ensure your controller is fully updated.

Gimbal Recenter:

What it does: Pressing this button instantly returns the camera to horizontal (0 degrees tilt), regardless of its current angle.

Why you'd want it: This is useful when you've tilted the camera up or down and want to quickly return to the horizon. Instead of manually rotating the left dial, you press a button and it snaps back.

How it feels: Press button → gimbal smoothly returns to horizontal in about 0.5 seconds.

Use cases: You were looking down filming a building, now you want to capture the skyline → press Gimbal Recenter. You were looking up at a bird in the sky, now you want to fly forward → press Gimbal Recenter.

This is such a useful function that it's the default C1 assignment.

Gimbal Point Down:

What it does: Pressing this button instantly tilts the camera to point straight down (minus 90 degrees), showing what's directly below the drone.

Why you'd want it: Overhead shots are valuable in aerial photography. With one button press, you can instantly switch from forward-looking to straight-down-looking.

How it feels: Press button → gimbal tilts to point down in about 0.5 seconds.

Use cases: Quick overhead map or inspection shots. Filming the tops of buildings. Getting a bird's-eye view of a subject. Filming something on the ground without moving the drone forward.

This is such a useful function that it's the default C2 assignment.

Auxiliary Light On/Off:

What it does: Pressing this button toggles an LED auxiliary light on or off (if your drone model includes one).

Why you'd want it: The Mini 5 Pro doesn't have a built-in auxiliary light, so this button is less relevant for your specific drone. However, if you ever use a different drone with lighting, this could be useful.

How it feels: Press button → light turns on (if off) or off (if on).

Use cases: Limited for Mini 5 Pro. This is more relevant for other DJI models that have built-in lights for low-light filming.

Note: Check if your specific Mini 5 Pro unit has an auxiliary light before assigning this button. Most standard versions don't.

Focus / Lock Focus:

What it does: Pressing this button locks the camera's autofocus on the current subject. Once locked, the focus doesn't change even if you move the drone or camera.

Why you'd want it: The Mini 5 Pro's camera autofocus is usually very good, but sometimes you want to ensure focus stays on a specific subject (like a person's face) even if the background changes. Locking focus ensures this.

How it feels: Press button → a focus lock indicator appears on the screen, showing that focus is locked on the center of the frame.

To unlock focus: Press the button again, or tap elsewhere on the screen.

Use cases: Recording a person in the foreground with changing backgrounds. Filming a moving subject where you want to ensure they stay in focus. Macro-style detailed shots where focus precision is important.

Note: The Mini 5 Pro's autofocus is usually so good that most beginners never need this function. It's more useful for advanced cinematography.

Advanced Customization

Holding C1/C2 + Rotating Right Dial = Control Shutter Speed or ISO (Pro Mode Only)

This is an advanced feature that requires your camera to be in "Pro Mode" (manual photography mode). Most beginners won't use this, but it's good to understand what's possible.

How it works:

While holding down C1 (or C2), rotate the right dial (the zoom dial).

Instead of controlling zoom, the right dial now controls a different parameter depending on your Pro Mode settings.

The most common parameters are:

Shutter Speed: How long the camera exposes light to the sensor. Slower shutter = more light, more motion blur. Faster shutter = less light, frozen action. Measured in fractions of a second (1/1000, 1/500, 1/100, etc.) or full seconds (1", 2", etc.).

ISO: The camera sensor's sensitivity to light. Higher ISO = more sensitive (good for dark conditions). Lower ISO = less sensitive (good for bright conditions). Measured in numbers like 100, 200, 400, 800, 1600, etc.

Why only in Pro Mode:

Pro Mode gives you manual control over camera parameters like shutter speed and ISO.

Standard photo and video modes have automatic exposure settings that the camera controls for you.

This advanced feature is designed for photographers who understand how shutter speed and ISO work and want fine-tuned control.

How to access Pro Mode:

In the DJI Fly app, on the main camera screen, look for a mode selector.

You should see options like "Photo," "Video," and "Pro."

Tap "Pro" to enter Pro Mode.

Once in Pro Mode, the camera is fully manual.

How to use it:

Let's say you want to adjust shutter speed:

In Pro Mode, you've configured C1 to control shutter speed.

Frame your shot.

Hold down C1 button.

While holding C1, rotate the right dial clockwise to increase shutter speed (faster exposure, less light) or counterclockwise to decrease shutter speed (slower exposure, more light).

Watch the shutter speed value on the screen change as you rotate the dial.

Release C1 when you've set your desired shutter speed.

The same process works for ISO if you've configured C1 to control ISO instead.

Practical example:

You're filming at sunset and want to intentionally blur motion (motion blur effect).

Enter Pro Mode and configure C1 to control shutter speed.

Hold C1 and rotate the right dial counterclockwise to a slower shutter speed (like 1/30 second instead of 1/60).

This longer exposure captures motion blur, creating a cinematic effect.

Important notes:

This feature is for photographers and filmmakers who understand manual exposure control.

Beginners should stick with automatic exposure modes until they understand how shutter speed and ISO affect images.

The Mini 5 Pro doesn't have the most advanced Pro Mode compared to higher-end DJI models, but it does offer manual control for creative photographers.

Practical Setups

Recommended Button Assignments for Beginners, Filmmakers, Photographers

Different types of pilots have different needs. Here are three proven setups that work well for different flying styles.

Beginner Setup (Recommended for Learning):

C1 Assignment: Gimbal Recenter

C2 Assignment: Gimbal Point Down

Why this works for beginners:

These are the two most useful gimbal functions when you're learning to fly.

Gimbal Recenter helps you quickly return to looking forward if you accidentally tilt the camera.

Gimbal Point Down lets you easily capture overhead shots, which are impressive and motivating for new pilots.

You're not trying to manage zoom or camera rotation while also learning basic flight control.

These assignments provide immediate value without overwhelming the learning curve.

Typical beginner flight: Take off, fly around with Gimbal Recenter as a safety button if camera tilts accidentally, press C2 for an overhead shot, land.

Filmmaker Setup (For Video Content Creation):

C1 Assignment: Camera Zoom (1x ↔ 2x)

C2 Assignment: Gimbal Recenter

Why this works for filmmakers:

Zooming in and out during flight is a common technique for establishing shots and detail shots.

Having zoom on a button (instead of rotating a dial) lets you zoom without taking your hands off the control sticks—you can zoom while flying.

Gimbal Recenter on C2 is a safety button if the gimbal gets accidentally tilted.

This setup lets filmmakers create dynamic shots with zoom changes while maintaining smooth flight control.

Typical filmmaker flight: Take off, establish scene with wide shot (1x), smoothly zoom in to detail (press C1), fly while zoomed in, zoom back out (press C1 again), capture more wide shots, land.

Alternative filmmaker setup:

C1 Assignment: Gimbal Point Down

C2 Assignment: Camera Zoom (1x ↔ 2x)

This variation prioritizes the ability to quickly get overhead shots while still having zoom accessible.

Photographer Setup (For Still Images and Aerial Photos):

C1 Assignment: Camera Rotation (Portrait ↔ Landscape)

C2 Assignment: Gimbal Point Down

Why this works for photographers:

Photographers often need to capture the same subject in both landscape and portrait orientations for versatility.

Camera Rotation on C1 lets you instantly switch between landscape (wider) and portrait (taller) framing without leaving the current location.

Gimbal Point Down on C2 gives you quick access to overhead composition.

This setup supports the compositional variety that photographers need.

Typical photographer flight: Arrive at subject, position drone, take landscape shot, press C1 for portrait orientation, take portrait shot, press C2 for overhead view, take overhead shot, land. All from the same location.

Alternative photographer setup:

C1 Assignment: Gimbal Recenter

C2 Assignment: Gimbal Point Down

This is simpler and works well for photographers who don't need camera rotation and prefer straightforward gimbal control.

Testing Your Custom Buttons

How to Verify They Work Before Flying

After assigning custom functions to C1 and C2, it's smart to test them before taking off. This ensures they work as expected and you're not surprised mid-flight.

Pre-flight testing at home (controller and drone powered on but grounded):

Step 1: Power on your controller and drone as usual (go through the startup sequence you learned in Chapter 6).

Step 2: Open the DJI Fly app and ensure you're connected.

Step 3: Position the drone so you can see it clearly. Don't fly it yet.

Step 4: While the app shows the live camera feed, identify the current gimbal position. Note what angle the camera is pointing (the app should show angle information).

Step 5: Press C1. Observe the response:

If C1 is set to Gimbal Recenter, you should see the gimbal move to horizontal. The camera should look straight ahead.

If C1 is set to Gimbal Point Down, the camera should tilt down.

If C1 is set to Camera Zoom, you might see a zoom indicator change (1x to 2x or vice versa).

Listen and watch: There should be a distinct sound as the gimbal motor moves, and you should see the camera move. If nothing happens, there's a problem.

Step 6: Press C2. Observe the response:

The C2 function should work distinctly differently from C1 (unless you assigned the same function to both, which is unusual).

Verify the camera moves or changes as expected.

Step 7: Test both buttons a few times:

Press C1 multiple times if it's a toggle (like Zoom). Verify it toggles correctly.

Press C2 multiple times to ensure consistent behavior.

Step 8: Listen for any unusual sounds:

Gimbal movements should be smooth and quiet (subtle whirring sounds are normal).

If you hear grinding, clicking, or loud squealing, there might be a mechanical problem. Don't fly until you investigate.

Step 9: Verify in the app:

Look at the on-screen gimbal angle indicator (usually shown in degrees or as a visual angle marker).

After pressing C1 (Gimbal Recenter), it should show 0° or horizontal.

After pressing C2 (Gimbal Point Down), it should show -90° or pointing down.

If the values don't match what you expect, double-check your button assignments in Settings > Control > Button Customization.

Testing during hover (optional but recommended):

If you've done the ground test and everything looks good, you can do a secondary test during a hover:

Take off to about 5 feet altitude in an open space.

Hover steadily.

Press C1 while hovering. Observe the gimbal movement.

Press C2 while hovering. Observe the gimbal movement.

This confirms the buttons work during actual flight conditions.

Return to ground safely.

What to do if a button doesn't work:

Verify the button assignment in Settings > Control > Button Customization.

Make sure it's assigned to a function and not set to "None."

Restart the app completely (force-close it and reopen it).

Restart the controller (power off, wait 10 seconds, power back on).

Restart the drone (power off, wait 10 seconds, power back on).

Try assigning the button to a different function, then back to your desired function. Sometimes a reassignment resets the button.

If it still doesn't work, it might be a hardware issue with the button itself. Contact DJI support.

Resetting to Defaults

How to Undo Custom Settings if Needed

If you customize your buttons and later want to go back to the original default settings, you can easily reset them.

Method 1: Manual Reset (Recommended for Changing Specific Buttons):

Step 1: Open DJI Fly app and go to Settings (⚙icon).

Step 2: Navigate to Settings > Control > Button Customization.

Step 3: For the button you want to reset:

Tap on "C1" or "C2."

You'll see a list of available functions.

Look for an option that says "Default" or "Reset to Default." Some versions might show the default function explicitly.

Step 4: Select the default option:

For C1: Select "Gimbal Recenter" (this is the factory default).

For C2: Select "Gimbal Point Down" (this is the factory default).

Step 5: Exit settings. The button is now reset to its default.

Method 2: Full System Reset (Reset Everything to Factory Defaults):

If you want to reset your entire controller to factory defaults (including all settings, not just button assignments), follow this process:

Step 1: On the DJI Fly app, go to Settings (⚙icon).

Step 2: Scroll down and look for "Advanced Settings," "System Settings," or "Restore Defaults."

Step 3: Tap on the option.

Step 4: You'll see a warning: "This will reset all controller settings to factory defaults."

Step 5: Confirm the reset by tapping "Reset" or "Restore Defaults."

Step 6: The app will process the reset (takes 10-30 seconds).

Step 7: All settings, including button assignments, gimbal calibration, and sensitivity settings, are returned to factory defaults.

Warning: Full system reset also affects other settings like gimbal sensitivity and stick sensitivity. Only do this if you want to reset everything, not just buttons.

Backup approach (if you're worried about losing settings):

Before making any major changes, take a screenshot or write down your current custom settings.

This way, if you accidentally reset something you didn't intend to, you have a record of what you had.

You can quickly manually reassign buttons to what you had before.

Why you might want to reset:

You realize a custom assignment isn't working well and want to start fresh.

You're experiencing button issues and want to clear any corrupted settings.

You're selling or giving the drone to someone else and want to restore it to a clean state.

You've made many experimental changes and want to simplify back to defaults.

Summary

You now fully understand the C1 and C2 custom buttons on your DJI Mini 5 Pro controller.

You know what the default functions are (Gimbal Recenter on C1, Gimbal Point Down on C2) and why those defaults exist.

You can navigate the exact menu path to customize buttons: Camera View > Settings > Control > Button Customization.

You understand six available custom functions in detail:

Camera Zoom (1x ↔ 2x switching)

Camera Rotation (Portrait ↔ Landscape)

Gimbal Recenter

Gimbal Point Down

Auxiliary Light On/Off

Focus / Lock Focus

You understand advanced customization using hold + dial for Pro Mode shutter speed/ISO control.

You have three proven practical setups:

Beginner: Gimbal Recenter (C1) + Gimbal Point Down (C2)

Filmmaker: Camera Zoom (C1) + Gimbal Recenter (C2)

Photographer: Camera Rotation (C1) + Gimbal Point Down (C2)

You know how to test your custom buttons before flying and troubleshoot if they don't work.

You know how to reset buttons to defaults if needed.

The C1 and C2 buttons are powerful tools for customizing your flying experience. Even though they come with sensible defaults, understanding how to customize them lets you tailor the controller to your specific flying style.

Chapter 10

Charging System

The Charging Hub

What It Looks Like, How Many Batteries It Holds (3), LED Meanings

The charging hub is your primary tool for charging batteries at home. It's a rectangular device designed to hold up to three batteries simultaneously, making it efficient for managing multiple batteries.

Physical appearance:

The charging hub is approximately 6 inches (15 cm) long, 2 inches (5 cm) wide, and 1 inch (2.5 cm) tall.

It's made of black or dark-colored plastic.

On the top surface, you'll see three battery slots arranged side by side.

On the bottom, there's a USB-C charging port.

The three battery slots:

Slot 1 (left): Accepts one battery. Has an LED indicator next to it.

Slot 2 (center): Accepts one battery. Has an LED indicator next to it.

Slot 3 (right): Accepts one battery. Has an LED indicator next to it.

Each slot is a vertical opening approximately 2 inches tall and 1 inch wide.

Batteries slide into these slots with the metal contacts facing downward into the slot.

LED indicators:

Each slot has a small LED light next to it.

These lights change color and blink pattern to show the charging status of the battery in that slot.

There may also be a master power indicator LED on the hub itself, separate from the three slot LEDs.

USB-C input port:

Located on the bottom of the hub.

This is where you plug in a USB-C charging cable.

The other end of the cable connects to a power adapter (5V-9V USB power adapter).

Power specifications:

Recommended input: 9V/3A (provides fastest charging, ~1.5 hours per battery).

Acceptable input: 5V/2A (slower charging, ~2.5 hours per battery).

Maximum input: Don't use chargers above 9V—they can damage the hub or batteries.

Charging One Battery at a Time

Inserting Battery, LED Progress Indicators, Removal

Even though the hub holds three batteries, you can charge just one. Here's how the process works step by step.

Step-by-step charging process:

Step 1: Prepare the battery.

Take a battery from your drone or from storage.

Inspect it visually for damage. If it looks fine, proceed.

Step 2: Prepare the charging hub.

Place the hub on a flat, stable surface (a desk or table is ideal).

Plug the USB-C cable into the bottom of the hub.

Plug the other end of the cable into a power adapter (9V/3A recommended).

The hub should power on. You may see an indicator light on the hub itself.

Step 3: Insert the battery into a slot.

Choose any of the three slots. You can use slot 1, 2, or 3—it doesn't matter.

Hold the battery vertically (contact end facing down).

Align the battery with the chosen slot opening.

Gently push the battery straight down into the slot.

You should feel and hear a click as the battery locks into the slot.

The battery should not wobble or move side to side. It should be firmly seated.

Step 4: Observe the LED indicator for that slot.

The LED next to your battery's slot should light up.

The color and pattern tell you the charging status.

See the LED meanings section below for what each color means.

Step 5: Wait for charging to complete.

A single battery typically takes 1.5 to 2 hours to fully charge (depending on power adapter wattage).

You can check the LED indicator to see progress.

The LED will change from blinking to solid green when fully charged.

Step 6: Remove the fully charged battery.

When the LED shows solid green, the battery is fully charged.

Gently pull the battery straight out of the slot.

If the battery resists, you can gently wiggle it side to side while pulling to release it.

Once removed, the LED for that slot will go dark (indicating no battery in that slot).

Step 7: Store the charged battery safely.

Place the fully charged battery in a safe location.

You can now insert another battery into the same slot to charge it.

LED progress indicators explained:

No light / Dark LED:

The slot is empty (no battery inserted), or the hub is not powered.

Verify the USB-C cable is plugged in and the power adapter is connected to wall power.

Solid green LED:

The battery in this slot is fully charged (100%).

You can remove the battery immediately or leave it in the slot.

Leaving a fully charged battery in the hub for extended periods is fine—the hub won't overcharge it.

Blinking green LED:

The battery is currently charging.

Battery charge level is between 50-99%.

The battery is charging normally.

Leave it in the slot and wait for the LED to change to solid green.

Solid amber / yellow LED:

The battery is charging, but slowly.

Battery charge level is between 0-49%.

The battery is in the early stage of charging.

This is normal when inserting a completely drained battery.

The LED will eventually change to blinking green as the charge increases.

Blinking amber / yellow LED:

Warning condition detected.

The battery may have a problem, or the power adapter may not be delivering enough current.

Possible causes: Low-wattage charger (like a 5V/1A charger), damaged battery, or temperature issue.

Try using a higher-wattage charger (9V/3A) if you were using a lower wattage.

If the problem persists, the battery may be defective.

Red or red blinking LED:

Error condition.

The battery cannot be charged due to a fault.

The battery may be damaged, over-discharged, or have internal damage.

Do not attempt to use this battery. Contact DJI support or replace the battery.

Fast Charging vs Trickle Charging

What Happens Using Different Wattage Chargers (9V/3A Recommended)

Different power adapters deliver different amounts of electrical current, which affects how fast your batteries charge. Understanding these differences helps you choose the right charger and manage your charging time efficiently.

Fast charging (9V/3A):

What it is: A high-wattage USB-C power adapter rated for 9 volts and 3 amperes of current.

Charging time: A single battery fully charges in approximately 1.5 hours.

How it feels: The charging process is noticeably faster. You can charge a battery in the morning and have it ready for afternoon flying.

Heat generation: The battery and hub may warm up slightly during fast charging, which is normal. This is why the hub has thermal management.

Recommended for: Fast-paced flying days where you need multiple batteries charged quickly. Recommended as your primary charger.

Benefits: Fastest charge times, enables quick battery rotation on long flying days.

Risks if overused: Frequent fast charging over extended periods (months) may slightly reduce battery lifespan. However, for normal use, this is acceptable.

Medium charging (9V/2A):

What it is: A 9-volt, 2-ampere power adapter.

Charging time: A single battery charges in approximately 2 hours.

How it feels: Still quite fast, but noticeably slower than 9V/3A.

Heat generation: Less heat than fast charging, as lower current is delivered.

Best for: Balanced approach. Good enough for most days, slightly easier on battery health than fast charging.

Slow charging (5V/2A):

What it is: A standard 5-volt, 2-ampere power adapter (like a typical phone charger).

Charging time: A single battery charges in approximately 2.5 hours.

How it feels: Noticeably slower than fast charging. On a long flying day, this can become limiting.

Heat generation: Minimal heat. The gentlest charging method.

Best for: Overnight charging or when you have time to wait. Extended lifespan preservation if charging frequency is very high.

Trickle charging (5V/1A or lower):

What it is: A very low-power charger, like an old phone charger or computer USB port.

Charging time: A single battery may take 4+ hours to charge, or may not charge effectively at all.

How it feels: Extremely slow. Not practical for day-to-day flying.

Hub behavior: The hub may show amber/warning lights because the power delivery is insufficient.

Best for: Emergency only. Not recommended for regular use.

Why charger wattage matters:

The batteries in your DJI Mini 5 Pro are intelligent and manage their own charging process.

The hub communicates with the battery to determine how much current to deliver.

A higher-wattage charger (9V/3A) allows the hub to deliver more current to the battery, charging it faster.

A lower-wattage charger (5V/2A) limits the hub to lower current delivery, resulting in slower charging.

Using a charger with insufficient wattage may trigger warning LEDs, even though the charging process might eventually complete.

Recommended practice:

Own at least one 9V/3A charger for fast charging during busy flying days.

You can use lower-wattage chargers (5V/2A) for overnight charging if you have time.

Avoid very low-wattage chargers (5V/1A) for regular use.

The 9V/3A charger is your best investment for efficient battery management.

Temperature effects on charging:

All chargers work best in temperature-controlled environments (room temperature, 50-77°F or 10-25°C).

In cold environments, charging slows down because the battery's chemical reactions are slower.

In hot environments, the hub may throttle charging to protect the battery from overheating.

For fastest charging results, charge in a cool room (not outdoors in summer heat).

USB-C Direct Charging

Plugging Into the Drone Directly When Hub Isn't Available

The Mini 5 Pro battery has a USB-C port, which means you can charge the battery directly without using the hub. This is useful for travel or emergency charging.

When to use direct charging:

You're traveling and didn't bring the charging hub.

You need to charge the battery while the drone is on, for emergency top-off power.

You want to charge just one battery and don't need the convenience of the hub.

How to charge directly:

Step 1: Remove the battery from the drone (if currently installed).

Step 2: Take a USB-C cable (the same type used for phones and modern devices).

Step 3: Locate the USB-C charging port on the battery.

The port is on one end of the battery (the end with the metal contacts).

There's a small opening protected by a rubber or plastic cover.

Step 4: Gently remove or slide back the protective cover if present.

Step 5: Plug the USB-C cable into the battery's charging port.

Step 6: Plug the other end of the cable into a power adapter (9V/3A recommended, 5V/2A acceptable).

Step 7: Plug the adapter into wall power.

Step 8: The battery's LED indicator lights should show charging status.

Solid green = fully charged.

Blinking green = charging (50-99%).

Amber = charging slowly (0-49%).

Step 9: When fully charged, unplug the cable from the battery.

Replace the protective cover if present.

Advantages of direct charging:

Portable: You can charge anywhere you have a USB-C charger.

One battery: Ideal if you're only charging one battery.

Direct feedback: The battery's built-in LEDs show charge status without needing to insert into the hub.

Disadvantages of direct charging:

Slower than hub charging: Direct charging is typically slightly slower than hub charging because the power delivery through the cable is less efficient than the direct contact in the hub slot.

One at a time: You can only charge one battery at a time (obvious, but worth noting compared to the hub which can charge three simultaneously).

Cable management: Requires keeping track of a USB-C cable and power adapter when traveling.

No hub overcharge protection: The hub has more sophisticated battery management. Direct charging relies solely on the battery's internal protection.

Charging times for direct charging:

With 9V/3A charger: approximately 2-2.5 hours (slightly slower than hub charging).

With 5V/2A charger: approximately 3-4 hours.

Direct charging in the drone:

You can also charge the battery while it's installed in the drone by plugging the USB-C cable directly into the drone's charging port (instead of the battery port).

This is convenient if the drone is stationary and you want a quick top-off without removing the battery.

However, this is slower than both hub charging and direct battery charging.

Use cases: Emergency top-off at a location before a second flight session.

Charging Indicators Explained

LED Colors, Blinking Patterns, What They Mean

The LED indicators on both the charging hub and the battery itself communicate the charging status. Understanding these indicators is essential for knowing when your batteries are ready to fly.

Hub slot LEDs:

Solid green:

Battery is 100% charged.

Safe to remove and use immediately.

Leaving a fully charged battery in the hub indefinitely is safe—it won't overcharge.

Can remain in the hub while other batteries charge in other slots.

Blinking green:

Battery is actively charging.

Charge level is between 50-99%.

Leave the battery in the slot until the LED changes to solid green.

Charging is proceeding normally.

Solid amber/yellow:

Battery is charging slowly.

Charge level is between 0-49%.

Battery is in early charging stage (normal when charging a depleted battery).

Will transition to blinking green as charge increases.

Charging will eventually complete, but it's taking longer than normal.

Possible cause: Using a low-wattage charger (5V/2A instead of 9V/3A).

If this persists for several hours, try a higher-wattage charger.

Blinking amber/yellow:

Warning condition.

Battery may have a problem, or charging conditions are abnormal.

Possible causes: Low-wattage charger insufficient for this battery, battery damaged, temperature extreme, or battery fault.

Troubleshooting: Try a different charger with higher wattage (9V/3A if you were using 5V/2A).

If warning persists with the correct charger, the battery may be defective.

Red or red blinking:

Error condition—battery cannot charge.

Battery has an internal fault or is damaged.

Do not attempt to use this battery for flying.

Contact DJI support or purchase a replacement battery.

No LED / LED off:

No battery is inserted in that slot, OR

Hub is not powered (check USB-C cable and power adapter connection).

Battery's built-in LED indicators:

Each battery also has four LED lights on the side (the same ones you pressed to check charge status manually).

These LEDs illuminate when you press the button on the side of the battery:

All four lights on = 100% charge.

Three lights on = 75% charge.

Two lights on = 50% charge.

One light on = 25% charge (low battery).

No lights on = Battery is completely discharged or has an issue.

These built-in battery LEDs are useful for quickly checking battery status without opening the app or inserting the battery into the hub.

Full Charge Time

Realistic Timing, Temperature Effects, Battery Degradation Over Time

Knowing realistic charge times helps you plan your flying schedule and battery rotation effectively.

Standard charge times (room temperature, 9V/3A charger):

Single battery in hub: 1.5 hours.

Two batteries in hub (parallel charging): Each takes approximately 1.5 hours (not doubled). Both finish at the same time.

Three batteries in hub (parallel charging): Each takes approximately 1.5 hours. All three finish at the same time.

USB-C direct charging (9V/3A charger): 2-2.5 hours (slightly slower than hub because of cable efficiency loss).

With 5V/2A charger (slower):

Single battery: 2.5 hours.

Multiple batteries: Each takes approximately 2.5 hours (parallel charging still works).

Partial charge times (useful planning):

0% to 50% charge: Approximately 45-50 minutes (faster initial charging).

50% to 100% charge: Approximately 50-60 minutes (slower final charging to protect battery health).

The slower final stage is intentional—the hub reduces charging current to prevent damage as the battery approaches full capacity.

Temperature effects on charging time:

Cold weather (below 50°F / 10°C):

Charging significantly slows down.

The same battery that charges in 1.5 hours at room temperature may take 3+ hours in cold conditions.

Chemical reactions inside the battery slow down at cold temperatures.

The battery's smart chip may actually refuse to charge if temperature is too low (below 32°F / 0°C) for safety.

Solution: Allow cold batteries to warm up to room temperature before charging. Bring batteries indoors before plugging in.

Hot weather (above 77°F / 25°C):

Charging speed is minimally affected, but the hub may throttle current to protect the battery from overheating.

Charging in a very hot environment (85°F / 29°C+) may take slightly longer as the hub reduces current.

Solution: Charge in a cool room or air-conditioned space. Avoid charging in direct sunlight or a hot car.

Room temperature (68-72°F / 20-22°C):

Ideal charging conditions.

Fastest charging times, optimal battery health preservation.

Best for all charging operations.

Battery degradation over time:

New battery (first 50 charge cycles):

100% of original capacity.

Fastest charging times.

Longest flight times.

After 100 charge cycles (approximately 3-6 months of regular use):

Battery retains approximately 95-98% of original capacity.

Charge times remain essentially the same.

Flight times are 95-98% of new battery times.

After 250 charge cycles (approximately 1-2 years of regular use):

Battery retains approximately 85-90% of original capacity.

Flight times are noticeably shorter (5-15 minutes less than new).

Charge times may be slightly longer.

Battery degradation is normal and expected. It's a property of lithium-polymer batteries, not a defect.

For heavy users (professional drone operations), replacing batteries annually may be worthwhile.

For casual users (occasional flying), a battery is good for 2-3 years of use before replacement is necessary.

Charging Safety

Not Overcharging, What Temperature is Too Hot/Cold, Fire Safety

Drone batteries are relatively safe compared to other power sources, but they do require careful handling during charging to prevent damage and ensure longevity.

Overcharging concerns:

Modern charging hubs have intelligent overcharge protection.

Once a battery reaches 100% charge, the hub automatically stops delivering charging current.

The battery is safe to leave in the hub indefinitely even after reaching full charge.

However, for battery health preservation, it's better to remove fully charged batteries from the hub after use.

Long-term health: Batteries kept constantly at 100% charge degrade slightly faster over time than batteries kept at 50% charge. This is why the optional "storage mode" exists (charging to 50% for long-term storage).

Best practice: Remove batteries from the hub after they reach full charge. Store in a cool, dry place.

Safe temperature ranges for charging:

Safe charging range: 50-104°F (10-40°C).

Below 50°F (10°C): Charging is very slow or may not occur at all. The battery's smart chip may prevent charging to protect battery health.

Above 104°F (40°C): The hub may throttle charging or stop to prevent overheating.

Below 32°F (0°C): Charging is not permitted. The battery's protection circuit disables charging.

Above 113°F (45°C): Battery may refuse to charge for safety reasons.

Freezing battery (below 32°F): If you accidentally charge a frozen battery, allow it to warm up naturally to room temperature first. Never apply external heat or place near a heat source.

Overheating during charging:

During normal charging, the battery may become warm (not hot) to the touch. This is normal.

A battery that becomes too hot to touch during charging indicates a problem.

Stop charging immediately if battery becomes very hot.

Likely cause: Battery defect, damaged internal cells, or exposure to extreme heat.

Contact DJI support; the battery may need replacement.

Fire safety:

Lithium batteries can catch fire or explode if severely damaged internally.

Prevent this by:

Never puncture, crush, or apply impact to a battery.

Never expose a battery to open flames.

Never immerse a battery in water.

Never charge a visibly swollen or damaged battery.

Never charge a battery that was dropped from a height or experienced impact.

If a battery is visibly damaged (cracked, swollen, leaking):

Do not attempt to charge it.

Place it in a safe, open area away from flammable materials.

Allow it to discharge fully on its own.

Contact DJI support for replacement or safe disposal.

Proper charging location:

Charge on a non-flammable surface (not on carpets or fabrics).

Charge in a well-ventilated area (not in closed cabinets or bags).

Keep batteries away from water and moisture during charging.

Charge in a room where you can monitor the process (not in remote locations).

Never charge unattended overnight (charge during daytime when you're awake).

Avoid charging during thunderstorms (power surges can damage the hub and battery).

Power adapter safety:

Use a genuine USB-C power adapter (9V/3A recommended) from a reputable manufacturer.

Avoid counterfeit or very cheap chargers that may not have proper current limiting.

Inspect the power adapter regularly for damage to the cable or connector.

If the power adapter ever becomes hot, smells unusual, or shows damage, stop using it immediately and replace it.

Multiple Battery Strategy

How Many to Buy, Charging Rotation for Long Shooting Days

As you increase your flying frequency, you'll want multiple batteries to maximize your flying time and keep the charging process manageable.

How many batteries to buy:

Minimum recommendation: 2 spare batteries (3 total including the one that came with your drone).

With 3 total batteries and the charging hub:

1 battery in the air.

2 batteries charging in the hub.

When the flying battery depletes, swap it for a fully charged one.

During the swap, the depleted battery goes into the hub to charge while flying continues with the fresh battery.

This enables continuous flying without waiting for a charge.

Recommended for regular pilots: 4-5 total batteries.

With 4-5 batteries:

Better battery health through rotation (no battery is overused).

Even more flexibility with charging schedules.

Can handle unexpected flight extensions.

Can charge in rotation without ever running out of flying batteries.

Professional/heavy users: 6+ batteries.

Continuous operation with minimal downtime.

Batteries can rest and cool between uses.

Optimal for commercial operations.

Recommended charging rotation strategy:

Three-battery scenario (1 flying, 2 charging):

Morning: Battery A is flying. Batteries B and C are charging in the hub.

Once Battery A depletes (after 20-25 minutes), land and swap it for Battery B (fully charged).

Battery A (now depleted) goes into the hub to charge (B and C are already charging, so now all three are available).

Battery B is now flying. Batteries A and C are charging.

After Battery B depletes, swap for Battery C.

Battery B goes into the hub.

Now Battery C is flying, and A and B are charging.

After Battery C depletes, swap for Battery A (now fully recharged).

This rotation continues indefinitely.

With the 1.5-hour charge time and 20-minute flight time per battery, you can achieve approximately 1.5 hours of continuous flying with only 30-minute breaks to charge.

Four-battery scenario (1 flying, 3 charging):

Morning: Battery A is flying. Batteries B, C, D are charging in the hub.

Battery A depletes in 20 minutes.

Swap to Battery B (fully charged). Battery A goes into the hub.

With three slots in the hub, you have maximum flexibility.

You can potentially have continuous flying all day if you rotate properly.

Five-battery scenario (rotation with rest):

1 battery flying.

3 batteries charging.

1 battery resting/cooling.

This is ideal because batteries can cool down between charges and flights.

Cooler batteries charge faster and maintain better health.

Practical tip for long shooting days:

Never deplete a battery to critically low levels (below 20%). Land and swap before it reaches critical levels.

Critical levels stress the battery and reduce its lifespan.

Ideal practice: Land at 30% remaining battery and swap to a fresh one.

The 30% depleted battery is safer for charging and less stressful on the battery cells.

Plan your flying sessions:

Morning session (1-1.5 hours): 3-4 flights using battery rotation.

Lunch break: While you eat, the hub charges the depleted batteries.

Afternoon session (1-1.5 hours): Another 3-4 flights using rotation.

Evening: All batteries fully charged and ready for the next day.

Battery as Power Bank

Using USB-C to Charge Phone or Other Devices From Battery (Shows Remaining %)

The Mini 5 Pro battery can double as an emergency power bank for your phone or other USB-C devices. This is useful when traveling or on long shooting days away from power outlets.

How to use the battery as a power bank:

Step 1: Take your Mini 5 Pro battery.

Step 2: Locate a USB-C cable (the same cable used for charging phones and other modern devices).

Step 3: Plug the USB-C cable into the battery's charging port (the same port you use when directly charging the battery).

Step 4: Plug the other end of the USB-C cable into your phone, tablet, or other USB-C powered device.

Step 5: Your device should begin charging immediately.

Step 6: To check the remaining battery percentage, press the button on the side of the battery. The LED lights indicate charge level:

All four lights = 100% battery charge remaining (full power bank capacity).

Three lights = 75% battery charge remaining.

Two lights = 50% battery charge remaining.

One light = 25% battery charge remaining (low power bank capacity).

This LED feedback is useful for managing the battery's charge as a power bank.

Charging capacity when using battery as power bank:

A full DJI Mini 5 Pro battery (2250 mAh) can charge a typical smartphone as follows:

iPhone 13: Approximately 50% charge (battery provides enough power to go from 0% to 50%).

Samsung Galaxy S21: Approximately 40-50% charge.

Google Pixel 6: Approximately 50% charge.

iPad or larger device: Approximately 20-30% charge (larger devices consume more power).

Practical example: Your phone is at 20% battery remaining. You're in the field shooting video with your drone. You plug the drone battery into your phone for emergency charging. The drone battery drops from 100% to 75% (one LED light lost), giving your phone another 30-40% of charge.

Why this works:

The battery has enough voltage and current to power most USB-C devices.

Modern phones and tablets support USB Power Delivery (USB-PD) charging, which the battery supports.

The battery's smart chip communicates with your device to deliver appropriate charging power.

Important considerations:

Battery wear: Using the battery as a power bank adds wear (additional charge cycles) to the battery. Use this feature only for emergencies, not for regular phone charging.

Prioritize flying: Remember that every percentage of battery you use to charge your phone is power you can't use for flying. Plan accordingly.

Charging slower than dedicated chargers: The battery will charge your phone, but more slowly than a wall charger or dedicated power bank. Expect 2-3 hours for a full phone charge using the drone battery.

Multiple uses drain battery quickly: Don't use the battery to charge your phone while the drone is actively flying. Your flying time will be severely reduced.

When to use battery as power bank:

Lost phone battery and need GPS navigation to get home.

Emergency communication when phone is dead.

Extended field work where you need phone backup power.

Traveling and forgot your phone charger.

Long filming days in remote locations.

What NOT to do:

Don't use the drone battery as your primary phone charger. That's what dedicated power banks are for.

Don't assume you can fly after draining the battery as a power bank. Always plan to charge it fully before flying.

Don't share the drone battery with other people regularly. The battery has limited charge cycles.

Summary

You now fully understand the complete charging system for your DJI Mini 5 Pro:

Hub charging: The three-slot hub charges batteries in parallel, with 9V/3A being the recommended fast-charging wattage (1.5 hours per battery).

Direct charging: You can charge batteries directly via USB-C when the hub isn't available (2-2.5 hours with 9V/3A charger).

LED indicators: You understand all the LED colors (green = charged, blinking green = charging, amber = slow charge, red = error) and what they mean.

Charging speeds: Different power adapters affect charging time (9V/3A is fastest at 1.5 hours, 5V/2A is acceptable at 2.5 hours).

Temperature effects: Room temperature is ideal; cold slows charging, heat throttles charging.

Safety practices: Proper temperature ranges, fire prevention, proper location, and damage prevention.

Battery strategy: Owning multiple batteries (3-5 recommended) enables efficient rotation and continuous flying without long waits.

Power bank use: The battery can emergency-charge phones and tablets via USB-C (roughly 50% phone charge per full battery charge).

The charging system is well-designed and foolproof for normal use. By following these guidelines, your batteries will stay healthy and provide reliable power for years of flying

Chapter 11

All the Cables, Connectors & What They Do

USB-C Main Cable

What It Charges (Drone, Controller, Batteries), Speed Differences

The USB-C cable is the primary charging cable for your DJI Mini 5 Pro ecosystem. It's the most versatile cable you own because it charges almost everything in your kit.

What the USB-C cable charges:

The drone main body: You can charge the drone directly by plugging the USB-C cable into the charging port on the drone's bottom.

The remote controller: The controller has a USB-C charging port on the bottom. You can charge the controller using the same USB-C cable.

The batteries: As you learned in Chapter 3, each battery has a USB-C charging port and can be charged directly via USB-C cable.

The charging hub: The hub's input port is USB-C, so the same cable powers the hub.

Why USB-C is used everywhere:

USB-C is the modern standard for charging devices. It's reversible (you can plug it in either direction), supports high-speed data transfer, and can deliver high wattage safely.

You likely already own USB-C cables for your phone, tablet, or computer, so you may already be familiar with it.

Physical description of the USB-C cable:

The connector end is small and rectangular with slightly rounded corners.

Approximately 0.5 inches (12 mm) wide and 0.3 inches (8 mm) tall.

Fully reversible—you can plug it in "upside down" or "right side up" and it works either way.

The cable itself is typically black or white and is flexible.

Standard length is approximately 3-6 feet (1-2 meters).

Speed differences (determined by power adapter wattage, not the cable):

The USB-C cable itself is the same regardless of charging speed. The speed difference comes from the power adapter on the other end of the cable.

5V/2A power adapter: Charges slowly (~2.5 hours for a battery, ~3-4 hours for the hub with three batteries).

9V/2A power adapter: Charges moderately fast (~2 hours for a battery).

9V/3A power adapter: Charges fastest (~1.5 hours for a battery, ~1.5 hours for the hub with three batteries).

Using a higher-wattage power adapter with the same USB-C cable results in faster charging because more electrical current flows through the cable.

Important safety note: The maximum recommended wattage for DJI Mini 5 Pro chargers is 9V/3A. Do not use chargers above 9V or with more than 3A of current, as these could damage the batteries or hub.

Cable durability:

USB-C cables are generally durable, but the connector can wear out over time with repeated insertion and removal.

If your cable stops working (not charging), try a different cable first to verify the cable is the problem and not the charging port.

If you need a replacement USB-C cable, any standard USB-C cable works with the Mini 5 Pro. You can purchase inexpensive USB-C cables from electronics retailers.

Pro tip: Keep multiple USB-C cables in different locations (office, home, travel bag) so you always have one available.

Micro-USB vs USB-C:

Understanding Your Cables, What Plugs Into What

While the DJI Mini 5 Pro uses USB-C exclusively, it's helpful to understand the difference between USB-C and Micro-USB (an older standard) in case you work with other devices or older equipment.

Micro-USB (older standard):

Physical appearance: Smaller and narrower than USB-C. Approximately 0.6 inches (15 mm) wide and 0.2 inches (5 mm) tall.

Directional: You can only plug it in one way. If you try to insert it upside-down, it won't fit. This is frustrating—many people remember struggling with Micro-USB on older phones.

Charging speed: Limited to 5V/2A typically (slower than USB-C's 9V capability). Maximum safe input is 5V/2A.

Where it's used: Older devices like older phones (Android before 2020s), older action cameras, older controllers, and various accessories.

Durability: The connector is weaker and wears out faster than USB-C with repeated use. Many Micro-USB devices failed because the connector would stop working.

Why it's outdated: The limitations (directional insertion, slow charging, weak connector) led to USB-C adoption.

For DJI Mini 5 Pro: You don't have Micro-USB. All your Mini 5 Pro equipment uses USB-C. This is modern and convenient.

USB-C (modern standard):

Physical appearance: Slightly larger and wider than Micro-USB. Approximately 0.5 inches (12 mm) wide and 0.3 inches (8 mm) tall. Slightly rounded corners on the connector body.

Reversible: You can plug it in either direction. No more frustration about "which way does it go?"

Charging speed: Supports up to 9V/3A (27 watts), which is much faster than Micro-USB.

Where it's used: Modern phones (iPhone 15+, Android devices, Samsung), tablets, controllers, many accessories, computers, and power banks. Industry standard for new electronics.

Durability: The connector is more robust and lasts longer with repeated use.

Data transfer: USB-C also supports fast data transfer (USB 3.1 speeds), not just charging.

For DJI Mini 5 Pro: All your equipment uses USB-C. You're using the modern standard.

Practical comparison:

If you have an older DJI drone (like Mini 2, Mini 3) with Micro-USB, you cannot use its Micro-USB charger with your Mini 5 Pro. You must use a USB-C charger designed for the Mini 5 Pro.

If you have a USB-C cable from your phone, you can use it to charge your Mini 5 Pro equipment (though you'll still need a power adapter that matches the Mini 5 Pro's 5V-9V requirement).

The takeaway: Don't confuse these connector types. Mini 5 Pro = USB-C only. If something says Micro-USB, it doesn't work with your drone.

Propeller Removal Tool

Yes, It Exists; Where It Is; How to Use It on Stuck Props

When you open your Mini 5 Pro kit, you'll find a small propeller removal tool. This simple tool is extremely useful when a propeller gets stuck and won't pull off by hand.

Where to find it:

The propeller removal tool comes in the DJI Mini 5 Pro Fly More Kit or standard kit.

It's usually located in a small compartment in the carrying case or in the accessories bag.

Physical description:

The propeller tool is a small plastic device, approximately 2 inches (5 cm) long and 1 inch (2.5 cm) wide.

It's usually light colored (white or light gray) plastic.

One end has a small flat blade or notch designed to fit between the propeller blade and the motor shaft.

When to use it:

You need to remove a propeller, but it won't come off by hand (it's stuck). This happens occasionally if the propeller was installed tightly and sits in direct sunlight (heat can slightly expand the connector).

A propeller that spun through water or mud may have dried and stuck.

How to use the propeller removal tool:

Step 1: Position the drone securely so it won't roll or slide.

Step 2: Identify the stuck propeller. Hold the motor shaft steady with one hand (don't let it spin).

Step 3: Take the propeller removal tool in your other hand.

Step 4: Locate the small gap between the propeller blade and the motor shaft.

Step 5: Insert the flat blade or notch of the tool into the gap.

Step 6: Gently apply leverage by pushing the handle downward. You're not forcing hard—just applying steady, gentle pressure.

Step 7: As the propeller begins to loosen, work the tool around the connector to break the seal.

Step 8: Once slightly loose, the propeller should be hand-removable. Pull straight up on the propeller.

Step 9: Once removed, inspect the propeller and connector for damage.

Important precautions:

Do not apply excessive force. If the propeller doesn't come off with gentle leverage, stop and try a different approach.

Do not let the motor shaft spin during removal. The spinning propeller can be dangerous. Hold the motor shaft completely still.

Do not drop the tool—it's small and easy to lose.

Do not use the tool on propeller blades. The tool is designed only for the connector area between blade and shaft.

Storing the propeller tool:

Keep the tool in your drone kit or carrying case.

If you lose it, you can purchase a replacement tool from DJI or similar tools from drone accessory retailers.

Having a backup tool is optional but useful if you fly frequently.

ND Filters

What They Are (Optional Accessory), How They Screw On, Why Professionals Use Them

ND filters are optional accessories that can significantly improve your video quality under bright lighting conditions. However, they're not essential for beginners.

What ND filters are:

ND stands for "Neutral Density."

An ND filter is a piece of darkened glass that screws onto the camera lens.

It reduces the amount of light entering the camera without changing colors or affecting focus.

Think of it like sunglasses for your camera—it darkens the image without changing the color tone.

ND filter strength levels:

ND filters come in different strengths, labeled by a number:

ND4: Reduces light by 2 stops (allows 1/4 of normal light). Mild darkening.

ND8: Reduces light by 3 stops (allows 1/8 of normal light). Moderate darkening.

ND16: Reduces light by 4 stops (allows 1/16 of normal light). Strong darkening.

ND32: Reduces light by 5 stops (allows 1/32 of normal light). Very strong darkening.

Which strength to use depends on your lighting conditions. Bright sunlight might call for ND16, while cloudy days might only need ND4.

Why professionals use ND filters:

Allows slower shutter speeds in bright sunlight: Without an ND filter, bright sunlight forces the camera to use very fast shutter speeds (1/1000 second or faster). This creates choppy, unnatural motion in video. With an ND filter, you can use slower shutter speeds (1/50-1/100 second) even in sunlight, which creates smooth, cinematic motion blur that looks professional.

Cinematic motion blur: The slower shutter speed creates motion blur in moving subjects, which filmmakers deliberately use for artistic effect.

Better depth-of-field control: Allows using larger camera apertures (though the Mini 5 Pro's aperture isn't adjustable, this principle applies to other cameras).

Consistent exposure: Prevents flickering when moving between sunny and shaded areas.

Why beginners might skip ND filters:

You don't need them to fly or record video. The drone works fine without them.

They're an additional expense (typically $30-60 for a set).

They're optional—your videos will be good without them.

They only matter if you're doing serious videography in bright sunlight.

How to install ND filters (if you get them):

Step 1: Remove the gimbal protector from the camera (if installed).

Step 2: Look at the camera lens. You'll see a ring around the lens.

Step 3: Take the ND filter—it's a small glass disc with threading on the edges.

Step 4: Align the ND filter with the lens opening.

Step 5: Screw the filter onto the lens by rotating clockwise.

Step 6: Tighten until snug, but don't over-tighten. You should be able to remove it by hand later.

How to remove ND filters:

Step 1: Gently grip the filter ring.

Step 2: Rotate counterclockwise slowly and carefully.

Step 3: Once loose, lift the filter off the lens.

Step 4: Store the filter in a protective case (usually comes with the filter set).

Important precautions:

Do not force the filter onto the lens. If it doesn't screw on smoothly, stop and inspect for misalignment.

Do not over-tighten, as this can damage the lens threading.

Keep the filter clean. Use a microfiber cloth to gently wipe dust off the filter glass before installing.

Store filters in a protective case to prevent scratches to the glass.

When to use ND filters:

Bright, sunny days when you want cinematic video with motion blur.

If you're shooting video in bright conditions and notice the video looks "stuttery," an ND filter can help.

Professional or semi-professional videography where cinematic look is important.

When you don't need ND filters:

Flying in cloudy or overcast conditions.

Taking still photos (ND filters affect video more than photos).

Flying casually for fun and not worrying about cinematic quality.

Budget is tight and you want to focus on essential equipment first.

Gimbal Protector

How to Put On/Remove Without Damaging the Camera

The gimbal protector is a curved plastic cover that shields your camera from impact and dust during transport and storage. You learned about it in Chapter 6, but here's the detailed guide on handling it properly.

Purpose of the gimbal protector:

Protects the camera lens and gimbal from scratches during transport.

Prevents the camera from being crushed if something falls on your drone in a bag.

Shields the gimbal from dust and dirt during storage.

Must be removed before any flight (the camera feed will be blocked if it's on during flight).

Physical appearance:

Curved plastic shell, approximately 3-4 inches (8-10 cm) wide.

Shaped to fit perfectly over the front of the drone housing the camera.

Has a pull tab or handle at the bottom for easy removal.

Usually light gray or white plastic.

Comes with the drone in the box.

How to put the gimbal protector on:

Step 1: Hold the drone steady, with the camera facing you.

Step 2: Take the gimbal protector in both hands, holding it at the sides.

Step 3: Position the protector directly in front of the camera.

Step 4: The protector should fit like a cap, sliding over the camera area.

Step 5: Gently push the protector forward and down, aligning it with the camera housing.

Step 6: Push until you feel it click or lock into place. It should sit snugly against the drone body.

Step 7: Tug gently on the protector to verify it's securely attached and doesn't wiggle.

How to remove the gimbal protector:

Step 1: Locate the pull tab at the bottom of the protector. It's a small notch or handle designed for your thumb.

Step 2: Place your thumb on the pull tab.

Step 3: Apply gentle, steady downward pressure on the tab while pulling the protector away from the drone body.

Step 4: Do not jerk or yank. Use smooth, consistent pressure.

Step 5: The protector should release smoothly and slide off.

Step 6: Set the protector aside in a safe place.

Important precautions:

Do not pull the gimbal itself. The gimbal is a sensitive component. Pull only on the protector's tab, not on the gimbal or camera inside.

Do not pull upward. Always pull downward and away from the drone. Pulling upward can stress the gimbal.

Do not force the protector. If it doesn't come off easily, stop and re-examine. You may be pulling at the wrong angle.

Do not lose the protector. You'll need it every time you pack up the drone. Keep it with your drone kit.

Inspection after removal:

After removing the protector, briefly inspect the camera lens.

The lens should be clear and free of dust.

If there's dust or a fingerprint on the lens, gently wipe it with a microfiber cloth before flying.

microSD Card

What Size Cards Work, How to Insert Correctly, Removing Without Breaking It

The microSD card is an optional accessory that stores screen recordings and data from the controller. It's not required for flying, but it's useful if you want to record what the controller screen shows during flights.

What the microSD card is:

A small memory card, approximately the size of a postage stamp.

Much smaller than a standard SD card (if you've seen those in cameras).

Stores digital data (video recordings of the screen, screenshots).

Capacity ranges from 32GB to 1TB (though very large capacities are expensive).

What size cards work:

Minimum: 32GB is the practical minimum. Smaller cards fill up quickly.

Recommended: 64GB or 128GB provides good capacity without excessive cost.

Large capacity: 256GB or 512GB cards work but are expensive. You probably don't need this much.

Speed class: For video recording, use "Class 10" or "UHS-3" cards for best performance. Slower cards may cause dropped frames.

Brands that work: SanDisk, Kingston, Samsung, and other reputable manufacturers work fine. Avoid very cheap generic brands with low ratings.

How to insert the microSD card:

Step 1: Locate the microSD slot on your controller.

The slot is on the bottom of the controller, near the USB-C charging port.

It's a tiny rectangular opening, approximately 0.5 inches (12 mm) wide.

Step 2: Take the microSD card. The card is very small, about the size of a small postage stamp.

Step 3: Orient the card correctly. The metal contacts (gold-colored side) should face downward into the slot.

Step 4: Align the card with the slot opening. The card will only fit one way due to the notch design.

Step 5: Gently push the card straight into the slot with steady, light pressure.

Step 6: Push until you hear a small click. The click indicates the card is fully inserted and locked.

Step 7: The card should be flush with the slot opening (not sticking out).

How to remove the microSD card (important: do this carefully):

Step 1: Gently push straight in on the card. You're not pulling yet—just pushing inward with light pressure.

Step 2: You should feel the card disengage and pop out slightly (about 1/4 inch or 5mm).

Step 3: Once the card pops out, gently grab it with your fingernails and pull it the rest of the way out.

Step 4: Do not yank or jerk the card. If it resists, stop and try pushing again to ensure it fully disengages.

Step 5: Once removed, store the card in a protective case to prevent damage.

Critical precautions (don't break your card):

Never pull the card out without first pushing it in to disengage the locking mechanism. If you try to pull it directly, you might break the card or the slot.

Never force the card. If it doesn't insert smoothly, you may have it oriented wrong. Remove it and try again.

Don't insert the card with power on. Though unlikely to damage anything, it's best to power off the controller before inserting/removing cards.

Don't let the microSD card get wet or dirty. Protect it in a small plastic case.

Don't drop the card. It's tiny and easy to lose. Keep it in a small protective case.

When the card is full:

If the controller storage is full, the app will show a message.

You can delete old recordings from the controller to free up space, or you can remove the card and replace it with a new one.

To prevent losing important recordings, periodically back up the card contents to a computer.

Spare Parts Kit Organization

How to Organize All Your Cables, Props, Filters in One Place

As you accumulate cables, propellers, filters, and other accessories, keeping them organized is essential. A disorganized kit means you'll lose small parts and waste time searching when you need something.

What to organize:

Cables (USB-C cables, power adapters).

Propellers (spare propeller sets).

Gimbal protector.

microSD card and protective case.

Propeller removal tool.

Microfiber cloth.

ND filters (if you have them).

Spare landing gear pads (if applicable).

Any other small accessories.

Organization options:

Option 1: Foam-lined carrying case (Recommended)

Use the hard-shelled carrying case that likely came with your drone.

The case typically has foam cutouts designed specifically for each component.

Place each item in its designated foam slot.

Pros: Professional, protective, everything has a place.

Cons: Limited to whatever case you have. If you need more space, you need a bigger case.

Option 2: Multiple small organizer bags

Purchase several small ziplock bags or fabric pouches.

Cables go in one bag.

Propellers go in another.

Filters in another.

Pros: Flexible, can rearrange as needed, inexpensive.

Cons: Small items can still get lost, not as protective as a hard case.

Option 3: Tackle box or fishing box

Use a plastic tackle box designed for fishing gear or tools.

These have multiple compartments and drawers.

Perfect for small parts.

Pros: Very organized, lots of compartments, affordable.

Cons: Not protective during travel, can be bulky.

Option 4: Specialized drone backpack

Purchase a drone backpack designed for DJI equipment.

These often have multiple compartments and organizational features.

Pros: Organized, protective, designed for drones.

Cons: More expensive than other options.

Recommended organization for beginners:

Start with the carrying case that came with your drone.

Place the drone in the main compartment.

Use the foam cutouts or side compartments for:

USB-C cables in a small ziplock bag.

Propellers in their original packaging or a small bag.

Microfiber cloth.

Gimbal protector.

Propeller removal tool.

microSD card in a protective case.

Power adapter in a dedicated pocket.

As you accumulate more accessories (ND filters, extra batteries, etc.), you can upgrade to a larger case or backpack.

Pro tips for organization:

Label everything: Use small labels or markers to identify cable types and propeller sets.

Keep original packaging: When possible, keep accessories in their original boxes. These are designed for safe storage.

Small pouches within the case: Use small ziplock bags or fabric pouches to keep tiny items (tools, cards) from getting lost in the main case.

Separate backup kit: If you fly frequently, consider keeping a second set of spares (extra propellers, cable) in a separate bag. If the main kit has an issue, you have backups.

Document your kit: Take a photo of your organized kit so you remember where everything is. This helps when packing quickly.

What You Absolutely Must Have

Essential vs Nice-to-Have Accessories

With so many accessories available, it's easy to overspend on things you don't need. Here's a clear breakdown of what's essential and what's optional.

Essential accessories (you need these):

Extra propellers: Propellers break from crashes. You absolutely need spares. The kit usually comes with 2-4 spares, which is the minimum. Buy at least one more set if you fly frequently.

USB-C cable: You need at least one cable for charging. Two cables are better (one at home, one in your bag).

Power adapter (9V/3A recommended): Essential for fast charging. At minimum, you need one; ideally, you have a backup.

Microfiber cloth: Essential for camera lens cleaning. Without it, you'll get dust and fingerprints on the lens, degrading image quality.

Carrying case or protective bag: Essential for transport and storage. Protects your drone from damage and keeps everything organized.

Why these are essential: You cannot operate the drone without power (cable and adapter), you will break propellers eventually (spares), and protecting your investment (case) and equipment (microfiber cloth for lens) is necessary.

Nice-to-have accessories (optional, but useful):

Extra batteries (2-3 total): Enables longer flying days without waiting for charging. Highly recommended for frequent flyers, optional for casual users.

microSD card: Allows recording screen data. Not essential—your drone works fine without it. Nice to have if you want to document screen activity during flights.

ND filters: Improves video quality in bright sunlight. Optional for casual users, valuable for serious videography.

Propeller guards: Protective cages around propellers. Nice for flying in crowded areas or around people, not essential for open-field flying.

Landing pad: A small mat that provides a clean takeoff/landing surface. Useful for landing on grass or dirt, but not required.

Spare gimbal protector: If you lose the original, a spare is handy. Otherwise, not essential.

Lens cap (if available): Protects the lens when not in use. Useful if you store the drone for long periods, but not essential.

Why these are optional: They enhance your experience or enable specific scenarios, but the drone works well without them.

Recommended starting kit for beginners:

1 extra set of propellers (beyond the spares that came with the kit).

1 USB-C cable (beyond the one in the kit).

1 high-quality power adapter (9V/3A).

1 microfiber cloth (for lens cleaning).

Your existing carrying case (likely came with the kit).

Total estimated cost: $50-100 beyond what's in the kit. This covers all essentials.

If budget allows, also add:

1-2 extra batteries (enables 1-2 extra flight sessions per day).

1 microSD card (64GB).

ND filter set (if you're interested in video quality).

Recommended upgrades after your first month:

If you fly frequently: Add 1-2 more batteries. This is the most impactful upgrade.

If you're interested in video: Add ND filters. They significantly improve cinematic video quality.

If you travel frequently: Consider a larger carrying backpack designed for drones.

What NOT to buy:

Cheap generic propellers from unknown sellers. Stick with DJI brand or well-reviewed alternatives.

Very cheap power adapters below 5V/2A. These either charge slowly or are potentially unsafe.

Excessive protective cases or redundant accessories. Keep it simple until you know what you actually need.

Gimmicky add-ons like propeller lights or custom skins unless you specifically want them.

Summary

You now understand all the cables, connectors, and accessories for your DJI Mini 5 Pro:

Cables: USB-C is your primary charging cable for the drone, controller, batteries, and hub. It's modern, reversible, and supports fast charging (up to 9V/3A).

Connectors: USB-C is superior to older Micro-USB (reversible, faster, more durable). Mini 5 Pro uses USB-C exclusively.

Tools: The propeller removal tool is a small plastic device for freeing stuck propellers without forcing them.

ND filters: Optional darkened glass filters that screw onto the lens to enable cinematic video with motion blur in bright sunlight.

Gimbal protector: Essential for transport/storage, but must be removed before flight. Remove via pull tab, install by sliding into place.

microSD card: Optional memory card for recording controller screen data. 64GB-128GB recommended. Insert carefully (contacts down), remove by pushing in first.

Organization: Use your carrying case or upgrade to specialty drone backpacks as your kit grows. Keep small items organized with pouches.

Essential vs optional: Essential items (propellers, cables, charger, cloth, case) are absolute must-haves. Nice-to-have items (extra batteries, ND filters, microSD card) enhance your experience but aren't required.

You're now equipped with knowledge about every cable, tool, and accessory you'll encounter with your drone. Next chapter covers the most critical topic: flight safety and regulations.

Chapter 12

Firmware Updates & Maintenance

What is Firmware?

Simple Explanation (Software That Makes Hardware Work)

Firmware is software that runs on your drone, controller, and batteries. Think of it as the "brain" of each device—it's the code that tells the hardware what to do.

The difference between firmware and regular software:

Regular software (like apps on your phone) runs on top of an operating system. Firmware runs directly on the hardware itself, embedded in the device's memory.

Firmware is permanent (or semi-permanent)—it doesn't disappear when you turn the device off.

Firmware controls everything the hardware does: how the motors spin, how the camera focuses, how the controller communicates with the drone, and how batteries charge.

Why your drone has firmware:

Without firmware, your drone's hardware would be useless—just plastic, metal, and electronics with no instructions for what to do.

The firmware receives your commands (move forward, take a photo) and tells the motors, camera, and other components how to respond.

The firmware also manages safety features like obstacle avoidance, altitude limits, and geofencing.

Why your controller has firmware:

The controller firmware translates your stick movements into signals the drone understands.

It manages the display, button functions, and wireless communication.

Why your batteries have firmware:

Battery firmware manages charging, discharging, safety, and health monitoring.

It's the "smart" part of the smart battery—it remembers charge cycles, monitors temperature, and protects against over-discharge.

You don't see firmware directly—it works silently in the background, making everything function properly.

Why Update?

Bug Fixes, New Features, Safety Improvements

DJI regularly releases firmware updates. Understanding why these updates matter helps you prioritize keeping your equipment current.

Bug fixes:

Bugs are software errors. A bug might cause a feature to work incorrectly or inconsistently.

Example: A firmware bug might cause the gimbal to occasionally jitter in video, or the controller might randomly disconnect briefly.

Firmware updates fix these bugs, improving reliability and performance.

If you experience a problem with your drone, checking for a firmware update is often the first solution. The update might include a fix for that exact issue.

New features:

DJI sometimes adds new capabilities through firmware updates.

Example: A firmware update might enable a new flight mode, add a new camera filter, or introduce a new gimbal control option.

These features allow you to do things with your drone that weren't possible before the update.

New features aren't critical (your drone works fine without them), but they can enhance your experience.

Safety improvements:

This is the most important category.

Safety updates improve collision avoidance, stabilization, or emergency landing procedures.

They might add geofencing for airport areas or improve GPS accuracy.

Example: A firmware update might improve the obstacle avoidance system's ability to detect thin branches or wires.

DJI takes safety seriously and releases critical safety updates whenever a risk is identified.

You should always apply safety updates promptly. Never delay a safety update.

Stability and performance:

Updates can make the drone more stable in wind, improve battery efficiency, or optimize motor response.

These improvements might seem minor, but they contribute to a better overall flying experience.

Telemetry and logging:

Some updates improve how the drone logs flight data or communicates with the app.

This data helps you understand your flights and troubleshoot issues if they occur.

How to Update

DJI Fly > Your Device > Firmware Version > Tap Notification > Update Button

The firmware update process is straightforward once you know where to look. Here's the exact path:

Step-by-step update process:

Step 1: Open the DJI Fly app on your mobile device.

Step 2: Ensure your drone and controller are powered on and connected to the app.

Step 3: On the home screen of the app, look for a navigation menu. This is usually at the bottom of the screen (tabs for "Fly," "Media," "Me") or accessible via a hamburger menu icon (three horizontal lines).

Step 4: Navigate to the section labeled "Me," "Profile," "Settings," or "Device" (exact name varies by app version).

Step 5: In this section, you should see "My Device" or "Device Management."

Step 6: Tap "My Device" or "Device Management."

Step 7: You'll see a list of connected devices:

Drone (DJI Mini 5 Pro)

Controller (RC 2)

Batteries (if applicable, depending on app version)

Step 8: To update the drone, tap on the drone from this list.

Step 9: In the drone's settings page, you'll see "Firmware Version" or "Software Version."

Step 10: If an update is available, you'll see a notification or a blue update button next to the firmware version.

Step 11: Tap the blue "Update" button or notification banner.

Step 12: The app will download the new firmware. This might take several minutes.

Step 13: Once downloaded, the app will prompt you to begin the update. Tap "Start Update" or confirm.

Step 14: During the update (10-15 minutes), don't turn off the drone or controller, and don't move away from the connection range.

Step 15: When complete, the app will show a success message. The drone will automatically restart if needed.

Updating the controller:

The controller firmware updates the same way:

In "My Device," select the controller (RC 2) instead of the drone.

Tap the firmware version to check for updates.

If an update is available, tap the update button.

Controller updates are usually faster (5-10 minutes).

Updating batteries:

Battery firmware updates are usually automatic.

When you insert a battery into the drone and power on, the system checks if the battery firmware needs updating.

If so, the battery updates automatically during the startup process.

You don't need to manually trigger battery updates in most cases.

Update Process

Don't Turn Off Drone, Don't Lose Power, How Long It Takes (10-15 Minutes)

The firmware update process is delicate. During the update, interruptions can cause serious problems. Here's what to watch for:

Time required:

Drone firmware: 10-15 minutes (most important update, takes longest).

Controller firmware: 5-10 minutes.

Battery firmware: 5 minutes per battery (usually automatic).

Total time if updating all three: 20-30 minutes.

Critical dos and don'ts:

DO ensure full battery charge before starting:

The drone must have enough power to complete the entire update without shutting down mid-process.

A power loss during update can "brick" the device (render it non-functional).

Always verify both drone and controller batteries are fully charged (100%) before starting.

DON'T turn off the drone during update:

If the drone turns off during update, the firmware installation fails.

A failed update can corrupt the firmware, making the drone inoperable.

The device will be stuck in an unusable state.

If this happens, you'll need to contact DJI support for repair or re-flashing.

DON'T interrupt the USB connection (if wired update):

Some older firmware updates required a USB cable connection to a computer.

The Mini 5 Pro typically updates wirelessly through the app, but if a wired update is ever required, don't disconnect the cable during update.

DON'T lose internet connection:

The app needs a stable internet connection to download and install firmware.

If your internet cuts out mid-update, the update fails.

Perform updates on a stable Wi-Fi connection, not mobile hotspot.

DON'T fly immediately after update:

After an update completes, perform a few test hovers before attempting serious flying.

The drone's behavior might be slightly different after a major update.

Verify that all systems respond correctly before flying normally.

DON'T manually shut down the device:

Let the device restart automatically if it needs to.

Don't force-quit the app or manually power off the device.

Allow the normal shutdown and restart process to complete.

What happens during the update:

The app downloads new firmware code from DJI's servers.

The code is transferred to the device's internal storage.

The device's processor installs the new firmware code.

The device performs a restart to load the new firmware.

The app verifies the update was successful.

Visual indicators during update:

You'll see a progress bar in the app showing update progress (0-100%).

The drone might make unusual sounds or movements as the system tests itself.

This is normal. The drone is not malfunctioning.

After completion, you might see brief LED blinking or controller vibrations as the system restarts.

If the update fails:

If an update fails, the most common cause is insufficient battery charge.

Try again with fully charged devices.

If it fails a second time, contact DJI support.

Do not attempt the update multiple times in rapid succession.

Battery Firmware

Also Updates Automatically, Separate From Drone Firmware

Battery firmware is unique because it updates somewhat independently from the drone firmware.

How battery firmware updates:

When you insert a battery into the drone and power on, the system checks the battery's firmware.

If the battery firmware is outdated, the system automatically updates it during startup.

Battery firmware updates happen in the background—you don't need to do anything special.

The update takes about 5 minutes per battery.

During battery firmware update:

The app might show "Updating Battery Firmware" or similar message.

The drone's propellers might spin briefly as the system tests motor response.

Don't interrupt this process.

The drone will not be available for flying until the battery update completes.

After battery update, the firmware version in the app will show the new number.

Battery firmware is separate from drone firmware:

Your drone might be on firmware version 1.5.2.

Your battery might be on firmware version 3.2.1.

These version numbers are different because they manage different things.

When you update drone firmware, battery firmware doesn't automatically update (though it should prompt if needed).

You should periodically update all components (drone, controller, batteries) for best performance.

Why battery firmware matters:

Battery firmware manages charge cycles, health monitoring, and safety protocols.

Outdated battery firmware might not recognize new safety features from the latest drone firmware.

Always ensure your battery firmware is current.

If you experience battery issues (won't charge, drains quickly, overheats), check if a firmware update is available.

Controller Firmware

Updates Separately, Done Through DJI Fly

The controller (RC 2) has its own firmware that updates independently from the drone.

How to update controller firmware:

Open DJI Fly app.

Navigate to My Device.

Select "Remote Controller" or "RC 2" from the device list.

Check the firmware version (should show current version and available version if update exists).

If an update is available, tap the update button.

The app will download and install the new firmware.

Controller update typically takes 5-10 minutes.

Don't power off the controller during update.

What controller firmware controls:

Button responses (how each button functions).

Stick sensitivity and mapping.

Display and screen functions.

Communication protocols between controller and drone.

Battery management (for the controller's own battery).

Custom button assignments (C1, C2 functions).

Why controller firmware updates matter:

Controller firmware must be compatible with drone firmware.

If you update drone firmware but not controller firmware, the two might be out of sync.

This can cause control lag, connection issues, or features not working properly.

Always update both drone and controller firmware together when updates are available.

Important: Update order matters:

Update drone firmware FIRST.

Update controller firmware SECOND.

Update battery firmware THIRD (or let it update automatically).

This order ensures compatibility.

If you update controller first and drone second, the devices might briefly be incompatible.

Cleaning Routine

How Often, What to Use (Microfiber Cloths), What NOT to Use (Water on Electronics)

Regular cleaning keeps your drone in peak condition and prevents dust from affecting performance.

How often to clean:

After each flight: Quick wipe of the lens and visible surfaces (2 minutes).

Weekly (if flying daily): Thorough cleaning of all accessible surfaces (10 minutes).

Monthly (if flying occasionally): Deep inspection and cleaning even if not flown regularly.

After flying in dusty conditions: Immediate cleaning to prevent dust settling into components.

Cleaning supplies you need:

Microfiber cloth (essential): Soft, lint-free cloth designed for camera lenses. Inexpensive and effective. You likely already have one from your phone or glasses.

Soft brush (optional): A small, soft brush can gently remove dust from crevices and landing gear. Avoid stiff brushes that might scratch.

Lens cleaning solution (optional): Camera-grade lens cleaning solution can remove stubborn fingerprints or dried water spots. Use only this solution, not household cleaners.

What to clean:

Camera lens: Most important. Dust on the lens directly affects image quality.

Gimbal area: Dust accumulation here can affect gimbal movement and responsiveness.

Motor shafts: Dry dust can be gently brushed away. Don't use liquid here.

Landing feet: These contact dirty ground. Wipe them clean to prevent dirt transfer inside the drone.

Controller screen: Clean with dry microfiber cloth. Screen is durable but treat it gently.

Propeller shafts: Wipe clean and dry to prevent corrosion.

How to clean the camera lens (most important):

Step 1: Power off the drone.

Step 2: Remove the gimbal protector.

Step 3: Look at the lens. Is there visible dust or fingerprints?

Step 4: If just dust: Use a soft brush to gently brush away loose dust. Or use the corner of a microfiber cloth to wipe very gently.

Step 5: If fingerprints or smudges: Use a microfiber cloth with a tiny drop of lens cleaning solution. Wipe gently in circular motions from center outward.

Step 6: If wet spots or water marks: Use a clean dry microfiber cloth to wipe them away. The solution will evaporate quickly.

Step 7: Allow to air dry completely (30 seconds) before reattaching gimbal protector.

What NOT to use:

DO NOT use water (unless specifically camera lens cleaner): Plain water can seep into electronics and cause corrosion. Only use dedicated lens cleaning solution.

DO NOT use paper towels or tissues: These are rough and will scratch the lens. Always use microfiber cloth.

DO NOT use household cleaners (like Windex or alcohol): These can damage lens coatings and electronics. Use only camera-grade products.

DO NOT use compressed air on electronics: Compressed air can force dust deeper into components. It's okay for lens, but not for motor areas.

DO NOT submerge in water: The drone is not waterproof. Keep water away from all electronics.

DO NOT use abrasive materials: No sandpaper, scouring pads, or rough cloths.

DO NOT apply excessive pressure: You don't need to scrub. Gentle pressure does the job.

Storage Maintenance

Monthly Checks If Not Flying, Looking For Corrosion, Battery Self-Discharge

If you take a break from flying, regular maintenance checks prevent problems when you return.

Monthly storage checklist (if not flying):

Battery health check:

Check the battery LED indicators. Press the button on each battery and observe the lights.

Lights should illuminate normally. If dim or non-responsive, the battery might have a problem.

Visually inspect for swelling or bulging. If a battery looks puffy, don't use it.

Corrosion check:

Look for white, green, or blue discoloration on metal connectors (battery contacts, charging ports, motor shafts).

This discoloration is corrosion—a sign of oxidation from moisture.

Light corrosion can be gently cleaned with a dry cloth. Heavy corrosion requires support.

Moisture damage check:

Check for water spots, white residue, or discoloration inside the drone.

Look around the camera lens for condensation or water spots.

If water got inside, the drone needs to dry completely (24+ hours in a dry environment) or professional service.

Movement and function check:

Power on the drone (5 minutes) without flying.

Verify all motors spin briefly during self-diagnostics.

Check that gimbal moves smoothly when you use the left dial on the controller.

Verify the camera feed displays on the app.

Listen for any unusual sounds (grinding, squeaking).

Propeller condition:

Visually inspect all propellers for cracks, bends, or damage.

Even if stored indoors, propellers can degrade over time.

If any are damaged, replace them before flying.

Battery self-discharge (natural phenomenon):

LiPo batteries slowly lose charge even when not in use.

A fully charged battery might drop to 90% after one week of storage.

After one month of storage, expect a 10-20% charge loss.

After two months, could be down to 50-60%.

This is normal and not a defect.

If storing for 3+ months without flying, perform monthly charging:

Charge each battery to 50% every three months.

This prevents deep discharge (which damages batteries) and maintains battery health.

A battery stored at 50% charge lasts longer than one stored fully charged or fully drained.

Storage environment matters:

Temperature: Cool (50-77°F / 10-25°C) is ideal. Avoid extreme heat or cold.

Humidity: Dry environment (not in a humid basement or bathroom). Moisture causes corrosion.

Light: Dark storage is fine (avoid direct sunlight, which can degrade plastics over time).

Stability: Store in a stable location where the case won't be knocked over.

Separated from hazards: Keep away from flammable materials, excessive heat sources, or corrosive substances.

When to Contact Support

Signs Your Drone Needs Professional Repair, Warranty Information

Not all problems require support, but some issues definitely do. Here's when to reach out to DJI.

Clear signs you need professional support:

Motor issues:

Motor won't spin during power-on self-diagnostics.

Motor makes grinding or squealing sounds (not normal whirring).

Motor spins unevenly (one faster than others, creating imbalance).

Battery problems:

Battery swells or puffs up visibly (dangerous, stop using immediately).

Battery gets extremely hot during charging (unusually hot to touch).

Battery won't charge at all even with correct charger.

Battery drops to 0% immediately after full charge (won't hold charge).

Red error lights on battery that won't clear.

Camera/gimbal issues:

Camera feed shows black screen despite gimbal protector removed.

Gimbal is stuck and won't move despite app commands.

Gimbal makes grinding sounds when moving.

Lens is foggy even after cleaning (internal condensation).

Connection problems:

Controller loses connection constantly (not signal—actual disconnection).

App crashes repeatedly during specific functions.

Drone won't recognize controller after re-pairing attempts.

Firmware issues:

Firmware update failed and device won't restart.

Device won't turn on after attempted firmware update.

Error message during update that persists after retry.

Physical damage:

Visible cracks in the drone body or arms.

Propeller won't install or remove even with propeller tool.

Water damage (water got inside despite precautions).

Corrosion that won't clean with dry cloth.

Problems you can usually fix yourself:

Connection drops: Try powering off and on, restart app, restart controller, try pairing again.

Slow charging: Verify you're using 9V/3A charger, check room temperature, ensure battery is cool.

Short flight time: This might be normal for older batteries or cold weather. Update firmware first.

Gimbal jitter in video: Often fixed by firmware update. Try recalibrating gimbal first.

Minor software glitches: Restart app, restart drone, restart controller (in that order) usually fixes.

Before contacting support:

Try these basic troubleshooting steps first:

1. Restart everything: Close app, power off drone, power off controller, wait 30 seconds, power everything back on, reconnect.
2. Update all firmware: Ensure drone, controller, and batteries are all on latest firmware.
3. Recalibrate: Go to Settings > Control > Gimbal Calibration. Perform recalibration.
4. Reset settings: Go to Settings and reset to defaults (backup your custom button assignments first).
5. Try a different battery: Swap batteries to verify if problem is battery-specific.
6. Test with another device: If available, try the controller with another drone or vice versa to isolate the problem.

Most issues resolve with these steps.

Warranty information:

Standard warranty: The DJI Mini 5 Pro comes with a one-year limited warranty.

What's covered: Manufacturer defects and hardware failures (the device doesn't work as designed).

What's NOT covered:

Accidental damage (dropping, crashing, water damage).

Intentional damage or misuse.

Normal wear and tear.

Damage from unauthorized repairs.

Damage from third-party batteries or accessories.

Extended warranty: DJI Care Refresh (purchased separately) covers:

Accidental damage.

Water damage.

Motor/propeller failures.

Battery failures.

2 years of coverage (with 2 claim incidents).

How to contact DJI support:

Visit support.dji.com

Live chat or phone support (available in many regions).

Email support (support@dji.com or regional equivalent).

Have your serial number ready (found on the drone body and in the app under "About").

Have photos of any physical damage.

Document any error messages exactly.

Describe the problem clearly and when it started.

Provide your region/country for regional support.

Summary

You now understand complete firmware and maintenance for your DJI Mini 5 Pro:

Firmware: Software that runs on your drone, controller, and batteries. It's the "brain" that makes everything work.

Why update: Bug fixes (improves reliability), new features (enables new capabilities), safety improvements (most important), performance optimization, and telemetry enhancements.

How to update: DJI Fly > My Device > Select device > Firmware Version > Tap Update. Don't interrupt, ensure full battery.

Update timeline: Drone (10-15 min), Controller (5-10 min), Battery (5 min, usually automatic).

Battery firmware: Updates automatically when inserted into drone. Updates separately from drone firmware.

Controller firmware: Updates same way as drone. Always update controller after updating drone for compatibility.

Cleaning: Use microfiber cloth on lens after each flight. Never use water on electronics. Clean weekly if flying daily.

Storage: Monthly checks if not flying. Watch for corrosion, battery health, and moisture. Charge to 50% every 3 months for long storage.

When to seek support: Motor issues, battery problems, camera/gimbal stuck, persistent connection loss, failed firmware updates, water damage, or physical damage. Most software issues resolve with restart and firmware update.

Warranty: 1-year limited warranty covers defects (not accidents). DJI Care Refresh covers accidental damage.

www.ingramcontent.com/pod-product-compliance
Lightning Source LLC
LaVergne TN
LVHW050647100826
845148LV00011B/2011
* 9 7 9 8 8 9 0 3 6 2 5 6 8 *